HALLOWEEN LAW

A Spirited Look
at the Law School Curriculum

Victoria Sutton, M.P.A., Ph.D., J.D.

VARGAS PUBLISHING

Copyright © Victoria Sutton 2012
victoria@victoria-sutton.com

Illustration and photography credits appear in the
Bibliography

ISBN-10: 0983802440 (paperback)
ISBN-13: 978-0-9838024-4-0 (paperback)

Manufactured in the United States of America
First printing, 2012
Typeset in the U.S.A.

Cover design and illustration by Summer S. Sutton

Published and distributed in North America by
Vargas Publishing
P.O. Box 6801
Lubbock, TX 79461
http://www.vargaspublishing.com

To my parents who introduced me to Halloween

To my teachers who introduced me to the law

To Summer and Remington
who introduced me to motherhood and my rights
and responsibilities for their Halloween costumes

Contents

Other books in this series by Victoria Sutton:

The Legal Kiss: The Legal Aspects of the Kiss (2011)

Winner of the Hollywood Book Festival Award,
Honorable Mention 2012

◉◉◉◉◉
Halloween Law: An Introduction

Halloween Law is an area of study which encompasses all the manifestations of Halloween including cemeteries, haunted houses, vampires, costumes, yard decorations and "trick or treat" outings. However, it might also be called National Say-or-do-what-I-have-been-secretly-thinking-all-the-rest-of-the-year Day from many of the cases and laws associated with Halloween. Halloween seems to be a day when permission is granted to act and think in a way that is otherwise not acceptable the rest of the year, making Halloween Law a fascinating subject for study.

The purpose of this book is to use Halloween Law as an introduction to the study of law, as well as a few advanced subjects, so you might also think of this book as an introduction to the law through Halloween. The First Year of almost every law school, otherwise known as the "1L" year, covers the general areas of the law --- property law, contract law, criminal law, constitutional law, tort law and civil procedure law. Some of the advanced courses taken in the second or third years of law school covered in Halloween Law will include a brush with Employment Law, Local Government Law, Oil and Gas Law, Legal Ethics and Health Law.

What might happen if someone sold a house and you didn't know that it was haunted? Or what if your neighbor decided to write your epitaph on a tombstone that he used for a Halloween yard decoration? Or what if someone took the vampire character too far in actually drinking blood from a victim? What if you got so frightened in a haunted house party that you broke your leg when you tried to escape? All of these fascinating questions span subject areas of law which will earn you the Letter in Halloween Law at the end of this book. At the end of this book, you may take the Halloween Bar Exam and upon successful completion, you will receive a Letter in Halloween Law, and the right to put "HL" after your name (if you dare).*

The U.S. Supreme Court Associate Justice, Antonio Scalia is the first and only Associate Justice to have said "Happy Halloween" from the bench, so don't believe for a minute that Halloween Law is not important to the U.S. Supreme Court. It happened during the oral arguments of *Central Virginia Community College v. Katz*, 546 U.S. 356 (2006) on Halloween, 2005. A light bulb blew out and made a loud gunshot-like sound. It triggered a spirited exchange between Associate Justice Scalia and Chief Justice Roberts. Here's the transcript:

> Justice ANTONIN SCALIA: Light bulb went out.
>
> Justice ROBERTS: It's a trick they play on new chief justices all the time.
>
> (Soundbite of laughter)
>
> Justice SCALIA: Happy Halloween.
>
> (Soundbite of laughter)
>
> Justice GINSBURG: That's the idea.
>
> Justice ROBERTS: Take your time.
>
> Justice SCALIA: We're even more in the dark now than before.

This makes Associate Justice Scalia the "father of Halloween Law".

So let's begin our survey with a short law quiz, provide some interactive entertainment and start to sort out all of these interesting Halloween activities into subject areas of law. This is a matching quiz. When you have finished, you can find the answers on the page that follows the quiz. Once you have gotten all of the answers correct (or after you have looked at the answers, whichever comes first), you will be ready to begin your study of Halloween Law.

    * Note: Please be aware that this course of study has no authority to grant any degree, title or license and you can sign your name any darned way you please, as far as this author is concerned.

Final Examination 1. Introduction to Halloween Law

Quiz Directions: Match the Halloween activity on the left with the area of law on the right in your first step to earning your letters in Halloween Law.

Halloween Activities	Areas of Law

Halloween Activities	Areas of Law
Cemeteries	Health Law
Epitaphs on Tombstones	Property Law
Vampire murders for blood	Contract Law
Yard displays	1st Amendment/ Constitutional Law
Blood donations	Legal ethics
Haunted houses	Criminal Law
Injuries from haunted houses	Employment Law
Lawyers looking for Halloween victims to represent	1st Amendment/ Constitutional Law
Local ordinances for public safety during Halloween	Local Government Law
Costumes at work	Personal Injury/ Tort Law
Costumes that are dangerous	Personal Injury/ Tort Law

Final Examination 1. Answers. Introduction to Halloween Law

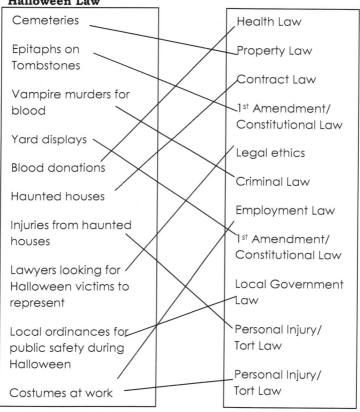

Cemeteries	Health Law
Epitaphs on Tombstones	Property Law
	Contract Law
Vampire murders for blood	1st Amendment/ Constitutional Law
Yard displays	Legal ethics
Blood donations	
Haunted houses	Criminal Law
	Employment Law
Injuries from haunted houses	1st Amendment/ Constitutional Law
Lawyers looking for Halloween victims to represent	Local Government Law
Local ordinances for public safety during Halloween	Personal Injury/ Tort Law
Costumes at work	Personal Injury/ Tort Law

Law School can be scary, but Halloween Law is just spirited fun. Enjoy your tour through law school. Moohahahaha.

5

2

๑๑๑๑๑
History of Halloween and Law

The idea of a holiday that has something to do
with the dead comes from All Hallows Eve, the Christian
holiday, immediately preceding All Saints Day on
November 1st. In the 8th Century, the Catholic Church
established the holy day, the "Feast of All Saints" to be
followed the next day with the "Feast of All Souls," or
those new Saints. A drab, barren time of year, the topic
was death and reflection on life. The day is from a
Catholic liturgy and was intended to recognize the Saints
and hold vigil for the dead the preceding night. Of
course this all evolved from pagan holidays to recognize
the dead, from many cultures, including the Britons who
saw it as the death of winter preceding the life of the
harvest, or the festival of Samhain. In Mexico, the Day
of the Dead is a major holiday also bridging the past
with the present Catholic religion.

Halloween Law in the United States may have
begun when around the end of the 19th Century it
started to appear to be a quasi-legal holiday because it
was being printed on calendars. The first case in
Halloween Law was in 1899, a vandalism case in
Nebraska. The first officially declared city celebration of
Halloween in the United States is said to have been in
Anoka, Minnesota in 1921. But by 1950 the tradition of
tricks had led to vandalism, a landmark development in
Halloween Law with the rise in vandalism laws. In the
21st Century a wave of sex-offender laws which applied
only on Halloween, became known as Halloween Laws.

The first book length history of Halloween in
America was, The Book of Hallowe'en (1919) by Ruth
Edna Kelley of Massachusetts, a historian. Then the first
book ever published on Halloween Law in 2012 (this one)
raised the spectre of an entirely new area of study for
law students and lawyers. Moohahahahaha.

Final Examination 2. History of Halloween and Law

1. Is Halloween believed to be an original pagan
holiday?
____yes ____no

2. Are people allowed to behave as if it is still the 8th
Century when the holiday was established?
___yes   ____no ____sometimes

Answers to Final Examination 2. History of Halloween and Law

1. The answer to the first one is *yes*. Halloween, or All Saints Eve was built on the original pagan holiday, Samhain in Great Britain and had lots of other names in other cultures. You probably got this one right whether or not you read your assignment. Sometimes professors give you a "freebie." But don't count on it.

2. The answer to the second question is *sometimes*. This is very good to get used to, because lawyers usually don't say *yes* or *no;* they usually say *sometimes* in response to almost every question. It is like the joke about wishing to find a one armed lawyer, instead of the usual lawyer who says, "on one hand the answer is yes and on the other hand it is no." *Sometimes* is almost always the right answer. But don't count on that easy choice after this one, without having to explain the *sometimes*, which is what lawyers do.

Congratulations! You have passed your introductory quiz on history. Now, on to the law school course topics.

3

●●●●●
Halloween Property Law

One of the first principles that is taught in property law is the simile of the bundle of sticks. Property possession or ownership is made up of rights which can be likened to a bundle of sticks. In some bundles you have ownership, mineral rights, and rights to build a skyscraper; whereas in other bundles you have only the right to possess the property for a limited period of time, as in a lease. So property possession and ownership can be different depending upon the type and number of "sticks" in the deed and covenants.

The property ownership with the most sticks is called ownership in "fee simple". If you think it sounds archaic, you are right. The term "fee simple" comes from the Dark Ages and the fiefdoms of Europe with landlords (another archaic term) and serfs and tenant farmers. In fact, the term "fee" is derived from "fiefdoms" which were rather complicated arrangements of military services and crops or goods delivered by the land holder to the landlord in exchange for use of the land and protection. It became a "fee simple" after the dissolution of fiefdoms and the complex obligations became, well, simple. There are other forms of land ownership which encompass fewer sticks in the bundle.

For Halloween, one of the important covenants (or stick in your bundle of sticks) is the one that allows for pumpkin patches or seasonal pumpkin sales on the property. This may seem rather innocuous, but pumpkin sales can generate quite a bit of traffic. A covenant that "runs with the land," as we like to say in law (which means the covenant is in the deed every time it is transferred), ensures that you can continue to sell pumpkins even if the neighbors don't like it.

In *Friends of Temescal Canyon, Inc. v. City of Los Angeles*, (June 29, 2005), a group of community

11

residents objected to the use of property for the seasonal sale of pumpkins during Halloween because they argued that it was inconsistent with environmental protection which was required for the permit to sell them. However, the court found that the Open Space Covenant which expressly (meaning in writing) included the seasonal sale of pumpkins, did not affect the future environmental effect on the property, because it was an existing use which had already considered for its environmental effects. The pumpkin patch was saved.

There are other important property law issues for Halloween, including those which involve cemeteries, graveyards and property ownership. So how does someone own a plot? Is it in fee simple, in perpetuity? Well that is what we like to think. But in fact, the plot is owned with only a right to use for burial as a kind of easement. An easement is a particular area within specific boundaries that can be used for limited purposes like walking or building a sidewalk for use by others. A burial plot is a kind of easement for burial with a specific rights holder. In some states, like New York, the right to transfer or sell the plot is limited to selling it or offering it first to the cemetery ownership [15 NYS §1513(c)]. Other states allow these plots to be sold on a secondary market ["Where Real Estate is Still Hot," *Wall Street Journal*, Sept 24, 2009]. Mortgaging is also prohibited in some states, like New York, because even if a bank foreclosed on the cemetery what would they do in a foreclosure?

You will never look at a cemetery the same, again.

Halloween Intellectual Property Law

Intellectual property law is an advanced course all by itself, but it is often introduced in first year Property Law courses. It turns out to be pretty important in Halloween Law, so here is an introduction to Halloween Intellectual Property Law.

Intellectual property has three distinct categories: trademark law, copyright law and patent law. A trademark protects "a word, phrase, symbol or design, or a combination of words, phrases, symbols or designs, that identifies and distinguishes the source of the goods of one party from those of others" according to the U.S. Patent and Trademark Office. A copyright protects an original art or literary work and a patent protects an invention.

At Halloween, the candy collected bears a trademark that assures the recipient that they have received a genuine treat of Snickers™, for example. Thus the trademark is useful in marketing, and so useful that companies will litigate any potential confusion with their trademark, if they perceive it to be diminishing their sales.

In Halloween law, a very important question arises in copyright law: Whether a Halloween costume can be copyrighted? Because of the unique design, anyone who has had their mother sew a Halloween costume for them, knows that such work is creative genius. Yet, clothing has historically been denied copyright or design protection. Things that can be copyrighted include "pictorial, graphic, and sculptural works," but the problem comes with the exclusion of things that are "useful", which cannot be copyrighted. Since costumes are clothing and therefore useful, they are not copyrightable. An exception exists when the design elements are completely separate from the clothing, but this is not the case with Halloween costumes. Thus, Halloween costumes are not copyrightable.

However, if you call costumes a "soft sculpture," can you copyright them? A company named Whimsicality wanted to copyright its unique costume designs, so it called them "soft sculptures" and avoided any reference to being worn as clothing by using photographs of the costumes lying on a flat surface rather than on humans. When Whimsicality tried to enforce its copyright against another company, Rubies which they claimed were making cheap versions of their copyrighted designs, Rubies objected to their characterization of the costumes as "soft sculptures" and called it fraud. Rubies claimed not only were Whimsicality's costumes not copyrightable, but Whimsicality had obtained their copyrights fraudulently by calling them soft sculptures.

All of this led to federal court at the trial level and appellate level, with different results, eventually resulting in the loss of the copyright once granted to Whimsicality.

So don't count on protecting the unique design of your Halloween costume that you or your Mom put together.

******

You are now ready to begin your first year property law final-exam-more-like-a-quiz. Most 1Ls find the thought to be a bit spine-chilling, but if you can avoid being spooked you can enjoy the ride.

Final Examination 3. Halloween Property Law

1. From where did the term "fee simple" in property ownership originate?
    - A. from lawyers' fees in property transactions
    - B. from medieval European fiefdoms
    - C. from the U.S. Constitution
    - D. from how simple property law is to learn

2. The "bundle of sticks" simile in property law refers to
    - A. the traditional way of passing ownership of property
    - B. the symbol of good luck in medieval days
    - C. the combination of rights that come with the property that describe how it can be used, possessed and sold
    - D. how to make a fire on your property

3. Is the right to use your property as a pumpkin patch one of the sticks in the "bundle of sticks"?
    - A. yes, but it may require other licenses or inspections
    - B. yes
    - C. no, no one wants a pumpkin patch in their neighborhood
    - D. no

4. Intellectual property law in Halloween costumes can raise an issue in
    - A. trademark law, because candy can be trademarked
    - B. copyright law, because clothing designs cannot be copyrighted
    - C. patent law, because patents are for inventions
    - D. none of the above

15

Answers
Final Examination 3. Halloween Property Law

1. From where did the term "fee simple" in property ownership originate?

The correct answer is B.
If you answered A, you have promise but you need to learn the law first. If you answered C, that is just because you haven't had that course yet. If you answered D, that is because you are just having so much fun with Halloween Law.

2. The "bundle of sticks" simile in property law refers to

The correct answer is C.
If you answered A, you might have dreamed it. If you answered B, you might want to consider a fiction writing as a career option. If you picked D, then you were clearly influenced by scouting as a child.

3. Is the right to use your property as a pumpkin patch one of the sticks in the "bundle of sticks"?
The correct answer is A.
While the right to use the property as a pumpkin patch is one of the "sticks" as a covenant in the deed, or a permitted use, it may still require environmental reports or local licenses. If you answered B, you are not wrong but it is not the best answer, and this gets you ready for the Halloween Bar exam which requires not just the right answer but the best answer. If you answered C, you may be right part of the time, but who can say? If you answered D, you are probably just engaged in wishful thinking about the pumpkin sales near your house.

4. Intellectual property law in Halloween costumes can raise an issue in:

The correct answer is B.
If you answered A, you are probably just thinking of the candy example. If you answered C, while the statement itself is true, it is not an issue in costume designs. If you answered D, then you probably just fell asleep in your allnighter studying for this exam and missed that section of Chapter 3.

Congratulations!
You have passed your Halloween Property Law Final Examination and can move on to your next course, Halloween Contract Law.

4

●●●●●

Halloween Contract Law

. . . as a matter of law, the house is haunted.
---- Stambovsky v. Ackley,1991

How many times have we had to sign a contract
for a cell phone, iTunes or cable television agreement
that would scare any ghoul on Halloween? Before we
could get our services, it had to be signed. Contracts are
a way of life in a complex world, where mutual
understanding in the beginning of a transaction reduces
conflict later when disagreements may arise. Quite
simply, a contract is a voluntary assent between two
parties with an obligation to pay or perform. *Black's
Law Dictionary*, the dictionary for law students and
lawyers, defines a contract as *an agreement between two
or more parties creating obligations that are enforceable or
otherwise recognizable at law.*

Buying a house can be pretty scary, too, and a
mortgage is a specific kind of contract that involves the
same basic elements of assent, obligation and
enforceability. But when you are buying a house that
turns out to be haunted, things can get even scarier.

That's exactly what happened in the classic
Contracts Law casebook case, remembered by many law
students as the haunted house case, *Stambovsky v.
Ackley*, 169 A.D.2d 254 (NY App. Div. 1991).

While it is true that the warning of *caveat emptor*
(let the buyer beware) is ensconced in the "as is"
language of a purchase of real estate contract, in
general; the failure to disclose defects may require the
seller to take back the property, and relieve the buyer
from the obligation to buy even after the contract is
signed. Under New York law, the seller had to either
have a duty or obligation to the buyer or actively engage
in trying to conceal the fault.

19

In this case, the court found that the buyer had truly promoted the idea that her house was "possessed", as the court called it. What may have been the nail in the coffin for the court was the note at the end of the Reader's Digest article by the seller, Helen Herdman Ackley, *Our Haunted House on the Hudson*, Reader's Digest, May 1977, which indicated she had been paid $3000 for verified claims of hauntedness. The court found that reputation was important to the value opining: *[T]he impact of the reputation thus created goes to the very essence of the bargain between the parties, greatly impairing both the value of the property and its potential for resale.*

Had the seller not taken this step of disclosing this fact to the public (once in a national publication, *Readers' Digest*, and once in the local press in 1977 and 1982, respectively), to which she owed no obligation, the court might not have found she owed an obligation to the buyer to disclose the claim of the house being haunted. The seller countered that she owed no such duty to the buyer and caveat emptor applied, but the court said simply that the seller was estopped, or prevented, from claiming she had no obligation to tell the buyer the house was haunted because she had gone to great lengths to inform the public of the fact. The court found that the house was haunted as a matter of law, but it did not find that the house was haunted as a matter of fact. So in the end, the law recognizes the house as haunted, without it having to be, in fact, haunted.

The court allowed the buyer to rescind the contract and avoid buying the haunted house. To do this, the court had to expand the exceptions to caveat emptor and opined, *It should be apparent, however, that the most meticulous inspection and the search would not reveal the presence of poltergeists at the premises or unearth the property's ghoulish reputation in the community. Therefore, there is no sound policy reason to*

deny plaintiff relief for failing to discover a state of affairs
which the most prudent purchaser would not be expected
to even contemplate (at 259).

In the court's opinion, you could see right
through the seller's failure to disclose and perhaps an
attempmt to try to sell the property for frightfully more
than it might have been worth, so the court lost no
opportunity to write a deservedly ghoulish opinion, as
follows, in part:

While I agree with Supreme Court that the real estate
broker, as agent for the seller, is under no duty to disclose
to a potential buyer the phantasmal reputation of the
premises and that, in his pursuit of a legal remedy for
fraudulent misrepresentation against the seller, plaintiff
hasn't a ghost of a chance, I am nevertheless moved by
the spirit of equity to allow the buyer to seek rescission of
the contract of sale and recovery of his down payment.
New York law fails to recognize any remedy for damages
incurred as a result of the seller's mere silence, applying
instead the strict rule of caveat emptor. Therefore, the
theoretical basis for granting relief, even under the
extraordinary facts of this case, is elusive if not ephemeral
(at 256).

The final part of contract law, the enforceability
element, requires a remedy and in contract, remedies
can be either money or action (to rescind or perform, for
example). These distinctions are known as either
remedies in damages or equity, respectively. The court
also saw this case as one not requiring money damages
but an equitable remedy which was to rescind the
contract to buy the house. The court made the decision
to carve a new exception in caveat emptor in New York,
though not as extraordinary as it would have been if
damages had to be calculated. To try to contemplate
how much money would compensate someone with a
haunted house would be to open another coffin of
worms, no doubt.

Final Examination 4. Halloween Contract Law

1.　A contract is an agreement between two parties
   A. that is legally binding
   B. that can be an agreement to agree
   C. that can be ignored if one party changes their mind
   D. that is not recognized in Halloween Law

2.　In the haunted house case, *Stambovsky v. Ackley,* decided applying New York law, normally the seller would not have been required to disclose any rumor about the house being haunted except that
   A. the seller forgot
   B. the seller had made a point to promote the house as haunted to the media and was paid for it, and thus was estopped from not disclosing it as a matter of law
   C. the seller had to disclose the haunted house fact because it was a matter of fact
   D. the seller wanted to haunt the house herself

22

Answers
Final Examination 4. Halloween Contract Law

1.   The correct answer is A
      A contract has to be legally binding or have legal meaning or it isn't a contract. It has to have obligations that are required by law, or anyone would take option C. Choice B is the classic example of what is not a contract, because it is also not legally binding if it is just an agreement to agree on something later. Choice D is simply not the case for Halloween Law since all of Halloween Law is directly useful and true for U.S. law and the state in which it is decided.

2.   The correct answer is B
The court found that the seller had made it a point to disclose that the house was haunted in a number of published articles about the house, making it impossible for her to say that it was not haunted, thus requiring disclosure as a matter of law. Choice C is not correct, because anything that is a "matter of fact" means that it is true, and who can say if the house was *really* haunted. It was just haunted as a matter of *law*.

      Congratulations!
      You have passed (or now know the answers to) the Contracts Law portion of your Halloween Law study. You may move on to the next subject, criminal law.

5

Halloween Criminal Law

One need not be a chamber to be haunted;
One need not be a house;
The brain has corridors surpassing
Material place.
Emily Dickinson

The basics of criminal law involve two parts or elements, the *mens rea* and the *actus reus*, both of which are required to be convicted of a crime. These are Latin terms which mean the "guilty state of mind" and the "physical act", respectively. So in murder, for example, there must be both (1) the requisite state of mind that the actor knew that his conduct would kill someone (*mens rea*), and; (2) the physical act or conduct must be evident (*actus reus*).

For the specific crime of murder in the Texas Penal Code, murder requires that the actor: (1) *intentionally or knowingly causes the death of an individual* (Texas Penal Code, 19 Vernon §19.02a).

In our look at criminal law, Halloween does not disappoint, with a vast array of cases. A number of Halloween related crimes, including murder, assault, vandalism, defacing a human corpse and principal to throwing a deadly missile. Vampirism may involve acts of drinking blood which could result in a finding of assault or the result of death of the victim. Trying to kill your vampire corpse in the neighborhood cemetery will get you arrested for defacing a corpse, regardless of your good intentions of killing a vampire. But let's start with the lesser crimes. Let's start with the "trick or treat", and here the "trick" is much tamer than the "treat".

25

The Trick. Vandalism

The Vandals were from a Germanic group known for senselessly defacing and destroying Rome in 455 A.D., and the derivation of the name of the crime, "vandalism".

Vandalism and tricks associated with Halloween may have roots in some behaviors of the post-Catholic Reformation period, 1500-1600s, when conflict was high with Catholics who were keeping the vigil of All Hallows Eve. Too much fun to give up, the tradition of tricks has continued.

But as with everything in society, there is a limit to the fun of tricks, and when the line is crossed it can result in a criminal penalty from a misdemeanor to a felony. A misdemeanor can result in jail time up to a year and a felony more than a year and usually this depends on the dollar amount of damage as well as any prior record. Egging and graffiti fall into the category of vandalism. Much more serious is the crime, Principal to throwing a deadly missile when deadly and objects are thrown from bridges onto vehicles, which can result in injury or death.

The Treat.

Historically, the treat was associated with the harvest of apples around the time of All Hallows Eve.

The tales of poisoned candy and razor blades in apples are mostly urban legend according to a study which spanned 25 years (1958-1983) of examining trick or treat incidents. The study found 76 police reports during that time, with only one case resulting from a father who intentionally poisoned his own son for the insurance award. The authors conclude that Halloween is not a holiday for sadists, but rather a result of "psychosomatic mass hysteria" caused by a fear of crime against children.

In 1975, Ronald Clark O'Bryan, an optician from Houston, Texas hatched a scheme to poison his son for insurance money by planting cyanide-laced Pixi Stix candy among his son's collected treats during his Halloween trick-or-treating. He also passed out more of it to other children in the neighborhood presumptively to cover up the source of the candy. Timothy, his eight-year-old son died hours after eating the candy. Fortunately, no other children ate the candy. In *O'Bryan v. State,* 591 S.W.2d 464 (Tex.Cr.App., 1979), Ronald Clark O'Bryan was convicted of capital murder. He was executed in 1984.

That is not the end of the gruesome tale, however, because Ronald Clark O'Bryan became known as the "man who ruined Halloween" and a song was written about him entitled, "The Candyman." This is as scary as any ghoul or vampire, and in some ways has replaced the things of which we are afraid at Halloween.

The Candyman,

Ronald Clark O'Bryan, "the man who ruined Halloween"

Photo, Texas Dept of Corrections

Here are selected lyrics from the song he inspired, *The Candyman* (Souixsie and the Banshees, *Tinderbox* album, 1985):

"...Sickly sweet, his poison seeks
For the young ones who don't understand
The danger in his hands

27

With a jaundiced wink see his cunning slink
Oh trust in me my pretty one
Come walk with me my helpless one . . ."

Trick-or-treat Murders at the Door

Knocking on the door of the wrong stranger can be deadly.

In Louisiana in 1986, Daniel Breaux, a 13-year-old boy, with a plastic machine gun was shot to death by the resident of the house where he rang the doorbell on Halloween night. The court found the following:

> *This suit arose from the unfortunate events of*
> *Halloween night in 1981. Jeffrey Scott Trammel,*
> *aged 15, Robert Martin Landry, Jr., aged 13, and*
> *Daniel Breaux, aged 13, went trick-or-treating*
> *that evening. About 6:30 p.m., Trammel and*
> *Breaux rang Robert Bouton's (plaintiff) front door*
> *bell while Landry waited at the sidewalk. Plaintiff*
> *opened the door and saw Breaux standing before*
> *him. Breaux was dressed in military fatigues and*
> *was holding a plastic model submachine gun.*
> *Plaintiff shut the door immediately and locked it,*
> *then armed himself with a .357 magnum pistol.*
> *He returned to the door, opened it, and saw a*
> *flash of light, caused, he alleges, by Trammel's*
> *triggering a photographic flash. Plaintiff's pistol*
> *then discharged, the bullet striking and killing*
> *Breaux. Bouton v. Allstate Insurance Co., 491*
> *So.2d 56 (1st Cir. 1986).*

Robert J. Bouton plead innocent and innocent by reason of insanity. His attorney argued that he was suffering from transient psychosis when the boys at the door appeared with fatigues and a plastic machine gun. The defendant was tried for second-degree murder and acquitted. (See Halloween Tort Law where Bouton after he was acquitted, sued the three boys for forcing him to defend himself in a criminal trial claiming they had assaulted him, provoking his response.)

Sex Offender Laws

Sex offenders have specially codified restrictions in Missouri, Louisiana and Illinois for Halloween, notably because Halloween is a holiday involving small children who go to houses in the dark – all conditions that may present sex offenders with opportunities they might otherwise not have to engage in repeat offenses, according to the state legislatures.

Other states have programs such as the State of California with "Operation Boo". In the District of Columbia, a joint task force of thirteen teams were dispersed to the 584 sex offenders in the District of Columbia on Halloween to make random checks on sex offenders at their home. The program included pre-Halloween counseling and a pledge signed by the sex offender that they would not receive children at their door or leave their home on Halloween.

In Orange County, California, laws passed February 2012 specified that registered sex offenders had to place a sign in the window specifying that no candy was at this residence on Halloween.

In *Doe v. Nixon* (Mo., 2008), the ACLU challenged the sex offender law which required, among other things, that a convicted sex offender must stay home during

29

Halloween festivities. Since some of the sex offenders were parents, they objected to being unable to go with their children for Halloween activities. The Missouri court struck down the state statute on the basis of Constitutional "vagueness" and for infringing on the liberty interest, one of the highest and most protected rights in the Constitution. The Fourteenth Amendment to the U.S. Constitution prohibits states from depriving "any person of life, liberty, or property, without due process of law . . . ." The "due process" also includes enough clarity in the law that a person does not know what is being required of him or her, thus "vagueness" would require the court to invalidate the statute. That is what the court did with regard to the Missouri statute.

Sex offenders will likely continue to be a focus of states during Halloween, as the possible consequences of not protecting children when they are vulnerable, in the dark of night visiting others' homes are indeed, scary.

Halloween as a Defense

There are three defenses in assault or murder which can be used in many state jurisdictions: Defense of self, defense of others and defense of property. If the response is deadly force, it must be proportionate to the attack, and in many states, defense of property is never a defense for a return of deadly force.

In 1898 Nebraska on Halloween night, a group of men decided to wreak mischief on a man who had borrowed a buggy and parked it beside his barn for the night. From about 10pm at night until 2 or 3am the next morning, the men harassed him about taking and destroying his buggy to which the man, Mr. Atkinson replied that he would shoot them if they took his buggy. A Mr. King finally took the buggy and made off with it, and Mr. Atkinson fired his gun and shot Mr. King in the leg.

The court found that the fact that it was Halloween was no defense for the men because *for, no matter under what name they may have masqueraded, the crowd was a mob, violating the law,* in *Atkinson v. State* (Neb., 1899).

Vampire Murders

Halloween Law must include some of the vampire activities which have led to some grizzly and gruesome results, particularly when blood is involved. Losing too much of it can result in death, and vampires don't always draw the line before going too far in depleting their victims.

Another type of vampire crime is using the defense that you were protecting yourself against a vampire. Whether killing a vampire or defending yourself against one, this all indicates where we should undoubtedly start in our examination of these cases --- the insanity defense.

The Insanity Defense

There are historically four tests for insanity in U.S. law, and it is helpful to take a quick tour through our legal history to nail down how these defenses developed to what we have to apply to modern vampire cases.

The insanity defense begins in modern U.S. legal history with the McNaghten rule from a British case which ruled on an assault on a man thought to be the Prime Minister of Great Britain (but was not). The court found "at the time of commiting the act the party accused was labouring under such a defect of reason, from disease of the mind, as not to know the nature and quality of the act he was doing, or as not to know that what he was doing was wrong" and thus the insanity defense was born.

The 1881 Parsons v. State case in Mississippi was the result of dissatisfaction with the McNaghten test, in that something more than a cognitive test was required. So the court developed the "irresistible impulse test," meaning that the person had no control over their actions. But it was still difficult to determine if someone was faking insanity.

The 1954 adoption of the New Hampshire insanity test, first used in 1871 there, seemed to make the test more specific because insanity had to be based on a mental defect or disease, but because the court did not define what a mental defect or disease might be, it quickly fell into disfavor and was abandoned by the U.S. Court of Appeals for the District of Columbia in 1971.

In 1962 the American Law Institute, which is made up of groups of member lawyers who address special areas needing clarification in the law, created an interpretation of the laws regarding insanity and developed a test that embodied all of the best of the insanity defenses. The test is as follows: . . .*a person is not responsible for criminal conduct if at the time of such conduct as a result of mental disease or defect he lacks substantial capacity either to appreciate the criminality of his conduct or to conform his conduct to the requirements of the law.* This allows both a determination of the intent as well as an expert opinion about the mental state of the defendant.

Then the Hinckley trial started a major reform movement for the insanity defense, when Hinckley was acquitted from attempting to kill President Reagan based on an insanity defense. Some states dropped the insanity defense all together, and others moved to reform it.

The Insanity Defense Reform Act of 1984 was the next attempt to once and for all find a solid way of determining insanity as a defense to a crime. The test under this statute reads:

> It is *an affirmative defense to a prosecution under any Federal Statute that, at the time of the commission of the acts constituting the offense, the defendant, as a result of a*

> *severe mental disease or defect, was unable
> to appreciate the nature and quality or the
> wrongfulness of his acts. Mental disease or
> defect does not otherwise constitute a
> defense. 18 U.S.C. §71 (2012).*

A verdict using this insanity plea is a "guilty but mentally ill" verdict.

In 1989, Michael Erickson was convicted of first degree murder which started with a plan to form a vampire cult with other friends. They plotted to kill one of their friends on a camping trip and they drank his blood --- rather, they licked it from their hands. (*State v. Erickson*, 449 N.W.2d 707 (Minn.,1989). His defense? The insanity defense. The court said they weren't buying the insanity defense, even if he had been delusional about forming a vampire cult. The court opined: *The ultimate inquiry, of course, is not whether the defendant is psychotic or has an antisocial personality but is, instead, whether defendant has proved by a preponderance of the evidence that because of mental illness or mental deficiency he did not know the nature of his act or that it was wrong.*

Recognize the insanity test? Sounds a lot like McNaghten Rule, doesn't it? Many states kept it.

Israel Herrera in Texas was sentenced to prison for stabbing his girlfriend to death because he thought she was a vampire and he needed to defend himself and others. So will the insanity defense succeed for Mr. Herrera? Here's what the court said about his expert witness who testified about his mental condition:

> *Dr. Estrada opined that petitioner was
> competent to stand trial. He also was of the
> opinion that at the time of the murder
> petitioner suffered from a psychotic
> condition that led him to believe that his
> girlfriend had been taken over by Satan and*

*transformed into a vampire and intended to
kill him and that he needed to kill the
vampire to defend himself and others. Dr.
Estrada thought petitioner thought that what
he was doing was right and did not know it
was wrong.*

So in Texas, the McNaghten Rule and the
irresistible impulse test is the insanity test. Israel
Herrera was sentenced to the Maximum Security Unit of
North Texas State Hospital in Vernon, Texas, where he
received treatment. He represented himself in an
unsuccessful appeal in *Cantu Herrera v. Dretke*, F.Supp.
2d (not reported), 2004 WL 3331891 (S.D.Tex.,2004).

In an appeal on Halloween 1980, a defendant
failed to convince the jury that he should succeed on an
insanity defense after setting his grandmother on fire. In
his conversation with his mother which was part of the
testimony, he described how he had prepared to kill his
grandmother and that , "I didn't stab her and didn't hit
her on the head like they said I did, but I then drank her
blood because, you know, I have to because that's what
vampires do, . . ."

The court did not find this met the insanity test
in Massachusetts in *Com. v. Riva*, 18 Mass.App.Ct. 713,
469 N.E.2d 1307, Mass.App.,1984.

There are a number of cases reported in news
sources which would indicate an insanity defense may
have been raised. Here are just a few of them.

Nathanial Chipps, Arkansas killed who he
thought was a vampire in self-defense.

Timothy White was arrested outside a church in
Jacksonville, Florida, March 2004, for killing a "vampire"
and said he was "vampire hunting".

In Colorado, Kirk Palmer, 28, killed Antonia
Vieira with a shotgun because he believed that Vieira
had turned his girlfriend into a vampire.

34

Probably not surprising that Halloween Criminal Law is fairly a long course and both the "trick" and the "treat" can turn criminal. Vampires and other ghouls can certainly bring out the worst behaviors in people. So did you discover whether judges accept Halloween as a defense for otherwise unacceptable criminal behavior? If you did, then you are ready for the Halloween Criminal Law Final Examination.

Final Examination 5. Halloween Criminal Law

1. Vandalism is a Halloween tradition that dates back to the 1500s, so it is not considered a crime on Halloween.

    ____true   ____false

2. The Candyman, known as the man who killed Halloween, was convicted of murdering his son with poisoned candy, because

    A. he had a motive (*mens rae*)
    B. he did the physical act of poisoning the candy and feeding it to his son (*actus reus*)
    C. he forgot to hide the evidence
    D. Both A and B

3. The insanity defense is important in Halloween Criminal Law because
    A. vampire murderers believe they are killing vampires
    B. a murderer can believe someone turned his girlfriend into a vampire
    C. a graverobber can believe he is killing a vampire
    D. all of the above

4. Sex offenders have special laws on Halloween in some jurisdictions, but in Missouri these laws were struck down as unconstitutional because:
    A. they violated their First Amendment right to speak to "trick or treaters" after dark
    B. the law was "vague" in terms of what could be criminalized
    C. the law infringed the liberty interest in the First Amendment
    D. B and C

Answers

Final Examination 5. Halloween Criminal Law

1. Vandalism is a Halloween tradition that dates back to the 1500s, so it is not considered a crime on Halloween.

    The correct answer is FALSE.

    In the case *Atkinson v. State* (Neb., 1899), the judge specifically noted that Halloween was not an excuse and a mob still violated law, despite the excuse that it was all in the name of Halloween.

2. The Candyman, known as the man who killed Halloween, was convicted of murdering his son with poisoned candy because

    The correct answer is D.

    It is necessary in any crime to have both A. he had a motive (*mens rae*); and B. he did the physical act of poisoning the candy and feeding it to his son (*actus reus*). If you answered with C, you should remember that this is a law course, not a television show.

3. The insanity defense is important in Halloween Criminal Law because

    The correct answer is D.

    All of these choices --- Choices A and B involve murders and C involves a lesser crime, but the insanity defense can be useful for all of them. Does it matter if the graverobber thinks he is killing but the person is already dead? Well, yes. In a murder, someone has to actually be murdered, no matter what the perpetrator thinks he has done. Remember, the state of mind and the act are both required.

4. Sex offenders have special laws on Halloween in some jurisdictions but in Missouri these laws were struck down as unconstitutional because:

The correct answer is D.

Choice A is incorrect because there is no First Amendment right to speak to "trick or treaters".

In *Doe v. Nixon* (Mo. 2008), the court held that the sex offender laws requiring parents not to leave their homes on Halloween night was void for vagueness and infringed the liberty interest protected by the First Amendment. So both B and C are correct answers, making D the right choice.

Congratulations!

You have passed Halloween Criminal Law, a frightfully important course for Halloween. You are ready to move on to Halloween Constitutional Law.

6

⚜⚜⚜⚜⚜
Halloween Constitutional Law

Constitutional Law encompasses the entire Constitution --- at least that is what is covered on the multistate bar examination. The Multi-State Bar Examination, or MBE, as it is affectionately known, is a set of questions about law that is the same for all states. Most state bar exams use the MBE as one of their requirements to be a member of that state's bar.

The first part of a typical Constitutional Law course is the structural aspects of Constitutional Law, including balance of powers between the Executive, Legislative and Judicial branches; separation of powers between the tribes, states and federal government and federalism. This would also include the Commerce Clause and all the other enumerated powers of the federal government. The second part of the course may typically cover the Bill of Rights, and for Halloween Law the First Amendment is particularly important.

The First Amendment is so important that the entire text of it should be read, especially for Halloween Constitutional Law:

Congress shall make no law respecting an establishment of religion, or prohibiting the free exercise thereof; or abridging the freedom of speech, or of the press; or the right of the people peaceably to assemble, and to petition the Government for a redress of grievances.
---U.S. Const., Amend. I

In Halloween Law, the First Amendment is full of concepts that are important to Halloween: the Establishment Clause, The Free Exercise Clause, Freedom of Speech, and the Right of the People to Assemble.

First Amendment, Freedom of Speech Clause

The First Amendment right to say things about your neighbors on tombstones in your yard as Halloween decorations is probably protected free speech. The Free Speech Clause reads:

Congress shall make no law. . . abridging the freedom of speech. . .

Free speech is one of the cornerstones of any democracy and the United States is one of the freest countries for speaking your mind. However, free speech is not without some constraints, even in America. Low value speech, commercial speech, hate speech, incitement to violence, obscenity and "fighting words" are all types of speech that can be limited but only by "time, place or manner" and possibly prior restraints. You have just been introduced to First Amendment free speech, which is enough for an entire course, but is typically covered in the first Constitutional Law course. In Halloween Law, the "fighting words" doctrine is dead on. Tombstones are where the words in question are written and it seems to be the preferred method of pushing the envelope with freedom of speech during the Halloween season.

Two cases are of particular import to our study of Halloween law, and they involve two different Halloween displays with words composed by their designers. The first is *Purtell v. Morton* which involved a protracted argument between neighbors over storing an 18-foot recreational vehicle in the driveway, to the consternation of several neighbors. After proposing that an ordinance be passed specifically to prohibit such eyesores, Jeff Purtell erected six tombstones, five of which had the names of the complaining neighbors with a tombstone-like message.

40

Purtell's display of tombstones.
Photo credit: From the published opinion.

Old John Burkuh
Said he didn'T give a care
So They buried hiM
aLive uP To his hair.
He couLdn'T breath
So now we're relieved
Of ThaT NasTy oLd jerk!
~ 1888 ~

The remaining tombstones read as follows:

~ 1610 ~
Dyean was
Known for Lying
So She was Fried.
Now underneath
these daisies
is where she goes crazy!!

~ 1680 ~
Roses are red.
Violets are blue.
There's stiLL
some space
Waiting for you!

BeTTe wAsN'T ReaDy,
BuT here she Lies
Ever since thAt night
She DieD,
12 Feet deep in this trench
TTT
Still wAsn'T Deep enough
For thAt wenches STench!
~ 1690 ~

42

Here Lies Jimmy,
The OlD Towne IDiot.
MeAn As sin even
withouT his Gin.
No LonGer Does he wear
that sTupiD Old Grin TTT
Oh no, noT where
they've sent Him!
~ 1690 ~

OLd Man CrimP
was a
GimP who couldn't hear.
SLiced his wife
from ear To ear
She died TTT He was Fried.
Now They're TogeTher
again side by side!
~ 1720 ~

CrysTy
wAs misTy-eyed
The DAy she DieD
AXE to the HeAD TTT
No DoubT She wAs DeAD.
Now There's no more
comPlain'n
Even When iT's rain'n!
~ 1860 ~

As the court describes them, "These inscriptions referred to neighbors Diane Lesner, Betty Garbarz, James Garbarz, and a neighbor who owned a crimping shop. The 'misty-eyed Crysty' referred to on the sixth tombstone was fictional; Jeff Purtell said he included this one to 'balance out' the display."

The court said that this was all protected speech, and the officer who finally made him take down the tombstones on threat of arrest was wrong. One court said he was immune due to his position of having to make law enforcement decisions on the spot. (It took the courts two tries to do the First Amendment analysis and they expected the officer to get it right on the spot, off the top of his head? The answer is yes, but in the end, he wasn't penalized.) So the case turned on whether the words on the tombstones were "fighting words."

The Fighting Words doctrine

A case referred to as *Chaplinsky* is the source of the fighting words doctrine, which was crafted as an exception to free speech when Chaplinksy stood on the steps of the courthouse and incited a fist fight, after bein told to by a police officer to stop. The principle has been shaped and sharpened in many cases that have followed, but it is still called the Chaplinsky fighting words doctrine. The rule from that case is an exception to unrestrained right to free speech, and speech under that doctrine that tends to incite immediate breach of the peace, is not protected. However, it has to be more than "psychic trauma", such as looking at obscene words on a t-shirt, because after all, you can look the other way. That is what the court said in *Cohen v. California* when he wore a t-shirt that said "Fuck the Draft".

The court in this case interpreted the "fighting words" doctrine as follows:

In law, "fighting words" are
abusive words or phrases (1) directed at
the person of the addressee, (2) which by
their very utterance inflict injury or tend to
incite an immediate breach of the peace,
that is, words that are likely to provoke a
violent reaction, and (3) play no role in the
expression of ideas.. .

So the court held that the tombstone inscriptions, though they may have caused psychic harm or fear, they did not rise to the level of fighting words and therefore were protected speech. Mr. Purtell's right to display these tombstones with these words in his lawn was protected by the court, and the officer was wrong to have forced him to remove the signs. However, the court did say that the officer was entitled to qualified immunity, having made the decision in the heat of the moment as a police officer.

Another case involved the placement of a sign depicting an insane asylum directional sign pointing to the neighbor's house, all in the spirit of Halloween.

Salama v. Deaton

Photo credit:
Jessica Vander
Velde

The case involved another long-running dispute between neighbors but even the dispute was disputed. Salama sold her house and sued Elizabeth Deaton for harassment and these photos were included in the motion.

Salama v. Deaton

Photo credit:
Jessica Vander Velde

It didn't end with these signs and tombstones. There was another which read: *"At 48 she had no mate no date/ It's no debate she looks 88."*

Without a published case, there is a reasonable chance the case was settled or dismissed.

The First Amendment is also important in expression in a parade as in *Grove v. City of York, Pennsylvania.* The plaintiffs, led by James Grove, are anti-abortion activists and their parade float was positioned at the end of the parade, for which they claim that their First Amendment free speech rights, free assembly and free exercise of religion were violated. These claims related to the 2004 and 2005 Halloween Parades held in the City of York.

It was alleged by the plaintiffs that the parade announcer said that "as Mayor Brenner had said at the beginning, [the York City fire engine] is being followed by something you may well not want your children to see, so this is basically the end of the parade. The last entry in the parade is entitled Dr. Butcher's Chop Shop, displaying the horrors of abortion and the wickedness of Halloween." In 2005, the plaintiffs' entry was entitled "Baby Disposal Service," and "three large signs depicting

46

aborted fetuses" were carried in the parade with the van "decorated with small coffins."

In a First Amendment, Free Speech analysis, the regulation cannot be content based. Speech can only be restricted because of time, place and manner if it is important to public safety, for example. The court opined, "A regulation on speech imposed because of the expected reaction by the people who hear it is, as a matter of law, content-based." The Plaintiffs argue that their float was placed at the end for exactly that reason – anticipated public response to their message, and thus was an impermissible regulation of content.

If there is a content regulation it can still be constitutional if there is a compelling state interest. In a First Amendment analysis for restricting free speech, the government has to have a compelling state interest that outweighs the right to free speech, which is a very high standard.

The court conducted that analysis and described the three-step test:

> The court must therefore conduct the strict scrutiny analysis to determine 1) whether the City had a compelling interest for taking those actions; 2) whether the City's actions were necessary to serve that compelling interest; and 3) whether there were less restrictive means available to the City that would have been effective.

The court found that the high standard was not met, and the court put the float at the end for "convenience" rather than public safety. So the court held the following: "Here, the City relegated Plaintiffs to the least-obtrusive location in its Halloween Parades, last, because it was the most convenient location for the City. Because this content-based regulation was not necessary to ensure public safety, placing Plaintiffs last violated their right to free speech. Summary judgment will be entered for Plaintiffs on this claim."

The court did not consider these to be fighting words at all, but it is worth mentioning that even a float in a St. Patrick's Day Parade of the National Socialist Party of America of people wearing Nazi uniforms and carrying flags with swastikas in a predominately Jewish neighborhood was considered not to meet the fighting words doctrine threshold to limit their participation in a St. Patrick's Day parade, even though it was home to many Holocaust survivors and had the potential to cause severe psychological injury. The court held this was protected speech.

The Establishment Clause

The Constitution prohibits the entanglement of religion with government, and so public schools may not be engaged in entanglement with religion. The Establishment Clause reads:

Congress shall make no law respecting an establishment of religion . . .

The school's Halloween party became a focus of an Establishment Clause action by Mr. Guyer in *Guyer v. The School Board of Alachua County, Florida.* He filed for a permanent injunction to prevent the school district from using specific symbols during Halloween celebrations because he claimed that the government was promoting a religion --- witchcraft, maybe? Here is what was in evidence:

[T]he affidavit of the principal of Hidden Valley Elementary School. . . stated that at the time in question, a number of teachers dressed in Halloween-related costumes, including a clown costume, a Ronald Reagan costume, and a witch costume; a member of the PTA put up a carnival poster which depicted a Halloween witch stirring a pot; some classes hold storybook dress-up day,

where the teacher dresses as a book character; on one occasion, a teacher dressed as the witch from The Wizard of Oz; the book Streganona, an award-winning fairy tale with a witch character, has been read in conjunction with the festivities; these activities have been displayed in a secular and non-sectarian fashion and there has been no attempt to teach or promote wicca, satanism, witchcraft or any form of religion; costumes and decorations simply serve to make Halloween a fun day for the students and serve an educational purpose by enriching the educational background and cultural awareness of the students. . . Included in the record is the school cafeteria calendar depicting a witch holding a wand, with the caption, "What's cooking?"

There is a three-part Lemon test (and yes, it came from the *Lemon* case) for the Establishment Clause which states that the government law or action:

(1) *must have a secular legislative purpose; (2) must not have the primary effect of either advancing or inhibiting religion; and (3) must not result in an "excessive government entanglement" with religion.*

The court held that the *mere depiction of witches, cauldrons and brooms, and related costumes, in context of public elementary school's Halloween celebration did not have primary effect of endorsing or promoting religion and, thus, did not violate establishment clause even assuming such symbols could have religious significance to followers of particular religion related to witchcraft; no religious ceremony was alleged to have occurred, and decorations served secular purpose of enriching children's educational background, cultural awareness, and sense of community.*

The Free Exercise Clause

Congress shall make no law . . . prohibiting the free exercise [of religion] thereof. . .

The First Amendment of the Constitution also prevents the government from prohibiting the practice of one's religion (unless it violates a criminal law, for example). Remember the parade case, *Grove v. City of York, Pennsylvania?* The plaintiffs, led by James Grove also claimed that the City was preventing the free exercise of their religion by placing their float last in the Halloween parade.

The test for a violation of the Free Exercise Clause is rather difficult to meet, and it requires that a law be specifically targeted at preventing the practice of a specific religion.

The actions taken by the City of York did not specifically target the religion practiced by the plaintiffs, nor did they prevent them from practicing their religion in any way.

The Right of the People Peaceably to Assemble

Mr. Grove in the parade case also claimed that his right to assemble was being violated when he was positioned last in the parade. This clause of the Constitution in the First Amendment reads as follows:

Congress shall make no law . . . abridging . . . the right of the people peaceably to assemble. . .

This right is so important that it has the same standard as Free Speech, which is that there must be a compelling state interest that outweighs the importance of the right to assemble. So unless there is a time, place and manner restriction, the right to assemble cannot be infringed and still be Constitutional.

In the parade case, the float was not prevented from being a part of the Halloween parade, and so Mr. Grove did not succeed on this issue.

Final Examination 6. Halloween Constitutional Law

1. Using Halloween decorations, can I express my feelings about my neighbor that I have held back all the rest of the year?

    A. Yes, and be sure and follow it with a good fist fight if invited.

    B. Yes, but only if I warn my neighbor that I am about to write something nasty about him or her on a tombstone.

    C. Yes, actually I could write the same thing any time of the year because my right to free speech outweighs any governmental interest in limiting it, as long as it does not fall into any of the categories that are exceptions to regulation and even then, I would probably not be completely prohibited from writing what I thought.

    D. No.

2. Using the fighting words doctrine, a limitation on the right to free speech

    A. would be based on an immediate fight because the fighting words were directed toward a particular person and caused violence.

    B. would cause a fight.

    C. would be constitutional.

    D. A and C

    E. A, B and C

    F. I don't know, I am completely confused!

3. As the city attorney, if there is a float entry in the city Halloween parade that is from an anti-abortion group (that is gruesome and bloody), the city can

    A. ban it because it is gruesome and bloody and the content is not suitable for the parade.

    B. ban it because the message is controversial.

C. permit it to be in the parade without any particular placement due to its message or gruesomeness.
D. place it at the end of the parade to allow people to leave before it arrives in their view.

4. The Establishment Clause means that the government cannot establish a religion by its activities, which would disallow:
A. displaying wicca symbols like a pentagram at public schools during Halloween
B. displaying pumpkins and witches at public schools during Halloween
C. allowing children to dress in costumes at public schools during Halloween
D. Definitely B and C, and I am not sure about A.

5. With regard to the Free Exercise Clause, when the anti-abortion activists in the case claimed the government was preventing them from practicing their religion because they placed their float last in the parade, the court held
A. no, the government did not prevent the practice of a religion because it did not specifically prohibit the practice of a religion by targeting the anti-abortion group religion or prevent them from practicing it.
B. yes, the government prevented the anti-abortion group from practicing their religion by placing the float last in the parade.
C. no, the government did not prevent anyone from practicing their religion by placing the float last in the parade.
D. no, but I don't know why.

6. The Right of the people to peaceably assemble was another claim in the Halloween parade case by the anti-abortion representative, Mr. Grove. If the city had infringed the right of the people to peaceably assemble then
A. the anti-abortion group would not have been allowed to have their float in the parade.
B. the anti-abortion group would not have been allowed to chant at the parade.
C. the anti-abortion group would have been required to buy a permit like everyone else.
D. the anti-abortion group would have been required to obey the public health and safety laws.

Answers
Final Examination 6. Halloween Constitutional Law

1. The correct answer is C.
While neighbors tend to chose the tombstone method of expressing their feelings and use Halloween as a good excuse, the principle is the same all the rest of the year for the right to free speech. Maybe Halloween is actually a therapeutic holiday for curing any reluctance to use your right of free speech?

2. The correct answer is D.
It could be A or C, but the best answer is D which includes both A and C. B and E are not correct, because using the fighting words doctrine itself does not cause a fight. Like that one? If you selected "F", you get half credit because the U.S. Supreme Court has had some difficulty in shaping the "fighting words doctrine" and hasn't been so clear about it themselves from time to time.

3. The correct answer is C.
Although some of the other answers may seem intuitive if you are trying to protect small children from the bloodiness or gruesomeness, the Court has opined that either A, B or D would be infringements on the Constitutional right to free speech. The entry in the parade would have to be allowed as long as they complied with the same rules and paid the same fees as everyone else.

4. The correct answer is A.
This is a tricky one, because you have to think about what the court said was allowed – pumpkins, witches, and all things secular. The court did not mention a pentagram or other Wicca symbols.

If you said D, that is understandable, because while not wrong, the correct answer A is the best answer of the four.

5. The correct answer is A.
The Free Exercise Clause is very specific and the government must direct its action specifically at a group's religion and prevent them from practicing it. So B and C are definitely wrong, although those actions were violations of the right to free speech. If you answered D, that would be alright if you were not studying law, but now that you are on the way to letters in Halloween Law, you should know why the answer is what you say it is.

6. The correct answer is A.
The correct answer is A because the prevention of the float being in the parade at all is the best answer for showing an infringement of the "right of the people to peaceably assemble." If your strategy was to pick B because there was not yet an answer with B, that is a bad strategy – your professors are on to that one.

Congratulations! You have passed Halloween Constitutional Law and are on your way to the last of your first year courses--- Tort Law.

7

⚫⚫⚫⚫⚫
Halloween Tort Law

Halloween is full of tarts, tortes and torts. Here, the Halloween Tort Law discussion is essential to Halloween Law because there are a lot of torts.

In general, tort law is the area of civil law that directs the tortfeasor to compensate the injured party when they have caused the injury, either intentionally or unintentionally.

What is a tort?

A tort is a civil wrong that is either intentional or unintentional, but may come from the same act as a criminal case (Remember the O.J. Simpson criminal case and then the civil case?). There are two categories of torts. The intentional torts are committed with intent. There are five general ones: assault, battery, false imprisonment, intentional infliction of emotional distress, and trespass. The unintentional torts include negligence and nuisance.

Each of these torts has a set of "elements" which all must be met in order to be proven in court. Tort law is state law, not federal law, but each state has the same basic elements for proving a tort. Mainly they differ in the way they determine liability. In civil cases the parties are called the plaintiff, which is the party suing or claiming to be injured and the defendant is the one who acted and against whom the case is brought. The burden to prove these elements is on the accuser, or the plaintiff. (Note that it is the complainant in criminal law, rather than the plaintiff, that begins a legal action, and it is the state in criminal law not the individual victim who actually brings the case.)

Not to keep you in the dark any longer, here are the elements of the five general intentional torts:

Assault has three elements. Intent will always be one of the elements in the intentional torts, and for assault the second is apprehension of harm and the third is causation.

Battery has three elements. First, an intent to commit a harmful touching; second, the action results in an actual offensive contact; and three, there is causation between the act and the touching.

False imprisonment has four elements. First, intent to confine the plaintiff; second, an actual confinement preventing the plaintiff from leaving; third, a causal link; and fourth, an awareness of the plaintiff of the confinement. The law of torts across the nation has been summarized and distilled into a general set of principles to help understand torts, called a "restatement". The Restatement (2nd) of Torts, §31, defines false imprisonment:
An actor is subject to liability to another for false imprisonment if:
(a) he acts intending to confine the other or a third person within boundaries fixed by the actor, and
(b) his act directly or indirectly results in such a confinement of the other, and
(c) the other is conscious of the confinement or is harmed by it.

Trespass to land also includes the element of intent, but it is a general intent of actually being on the land, perhaps without knowing one is trespassing. The Restatement (2nd) of Torts, section 329, states: A trespasser is a person who enters or remains upon land in the possession of another without a privilege to do so created by the possessor's consent or otherwise.
There are several other kinds of trespass, too.

Intentional infliction of emotional distress has four elements: 1. intent to cause or reckless disregard or the probability of causing emotional distress; 2. outrageous conduct by the defendant; 3. actual damages or suffering; and 4. causation of the emotional distress by the plaintiff's outrageous conduct.

The Unintentional torts

The unintentional torts lack the common element of intent, but the general concept is that although intent may not be present, the extent of the recklessness, carelessness or neglect may give rise to a wrong that should be compensated because of these actions. Negligence and product liability are unintentional torts.

For **negligence,** first, there must be a duty to the plaintiff; second that duty must have been breached by the defendant; third, there must be a link between the injuries and the acts of the defendant, called "proximate cause" and the risk has to be a foreseeable one; fourth, the plaintiff must have suffered damages as a result of all of the above.

There are some defenses like assumption of risk, attractive nuisance and consent which arise in Halloween Tort Law and can help a defendant.

Product liability is the result of a product that has either a design defect, a manufacturing defect or a marketing defect that renders it strictly liable for the harm it causes. The strict liability standard means that it does not matter how careful the manufacturer was in the process, the mere production of it makes the manufacturer strictly liable for the harm.

Defenses to product liability could be statutorily created or if the product is used in a way that was clearly not intended.

Now that the basics of tort law are firmly locked in your mind, you are ready to begin the scary tour through haunted houses, Halloween costumes and just plain human behavior on that special day of the year when people do things they would never do any other day of the year.

Negligence in Haunted Houses and Corn Mazes

Haunted Houses are particularly good places to have accidents --- they need to be dark so that patrons cannot see and they are filled with scary actors and situations which may cause reactions that result in self-injury or unintentional injuries. The people who work as the actors can also be injured.

A negligence case begins with the question of duty. Does the haunted house owner owe a duty to the patron? If so, what is that duty? The patron rightfully expects not to be faced with an unreasonable danger, but they do expect to have a frightening experience. In fact, they are paying to be frightened in a haunted house, which alters the normal duty "not to scare" another. The court described this "modified duty" on Halloween:

> On any other evening, presenting a frightening or threatening visage might be a violation of a general duty not to scare others. But on Halloween at trick-or-treat time, that duty is modified. Our society encourages children to transform themselves into witches, demons, and ghosts, and play a game of threatening neighbors into giving them candy.
> Bouton v. Allstate Ins. Co., 491 So. 2d 56, 59 (La. Ct. App. 1986).

The court has held that haunted houses are typically not unreasonable risks. Patrons who enter a haunted house assume the risk of things that typically happen in

60

a haunted house, including their own actions when they are frightened.

In *Durman* (La. App. Ct.), a chainsaw actor ran after a patron of a corn maze, who heard the chainsaw and ran, slipped in the mud and was injuried, but the court held the mud was part of being in a corn maze. The court said, "Accordingly, we find that no duty was owed by the Billingses to Mrs. Durmon in this case to warn or protect her from her reaction to being frightened by "Jason," an experience she expected to have and for which she paid an additional admission fee." *In Mays v. Gretna* (La.App., 5th Cir.1996)where a patron was injured who ran into a brick wall after being frightened; and in *Bonanno v. Continental*, where a devil frightened patrons their assumption of the risk of being frightened was a complete defense to these negligence cases against the haunted houses. In all three cases, the courts held that these were not unreasonable risks and there was no duty to guard against fright resulting from a haunted house, because after all, that is what patrons paid for.

In *Policeman's Benefit Association*, the security guard shoved a patron against the wall, injuring them, which was not a risk the patron had assumed. The only question was whether the act had been reckless (not simply negligent) which would decide whether the insurance company would defend the guard. In *Powell*, a patron claimed she suffered a mental disability as neurological disorders after visiting the haunted house in Lexington, Kentucky and receiving a blow to the head by a "ghost". In *Seipp*, a patron was injured while attending a haunted house that was owned by the school district. Because the school district had not properly completed the requirements to rent the facility to the organization, the court did not grant its usual sovereign immunity making the school liable for the patrons' injuries.

The court has held that haunted house establishments do not owe a duty to protect patrons from traffic after they leave the house. In *Arthur* (La.), a patron was injured in traffic after leaving the haunted house and the court held that the haunted house had no duty to patrons after they left the house and so no negligence. Also, in *Galan*, a patron was injured while leaving the haunted house and the court held there was no breach of duty.

However, where a haunted house did not have a firefighter present to assist a patron who was injured on a slide in the haunted house, the court held the haunted house had breached its duty to protect its patrons from unreasonable risks, in *Burton*. The court found negligence. In *Holman* (Ill.), a grandma was visiting a Halloween display in the Illinois State Museum with her grandson, the lights were out, and she fell over some chairs piled in the corner of the room. It was distinguishable from the other cases where there is no duty "not to scare" because here, the haunted house had been unreasonable. A pile of chairs in a corner presented an unreasonable risk and the haunted house had a duty to protect the patrons from such unreasonable risks. The court held the house was negligent and breached their duty of reasonable care to the grandma.

Some states require a contributory negligence formulation. If the patron contributed to the negligence they may have no recovery or they may have a proportionate recover depending on the percentage of the negligence the court attributes to them. This is a state law which varies from state to state.

Haunted Houses as Attractive Nuisances

An attractive nuisance is a defense in a trespass in land claim. An attractive nuisance is an exception to the trespass rule that landowners owe no duty to trespassers except willful and wanton harm. The elements of attractive nuisance require (1) that a potentially dangerous condition exists on the property;

(2) that the landowner created or maintained the potential hazard; (3) that the landowner should have known the condition would attract children; and (4) that the landowner should have known the condition could harm children.

In *Hayward v. Carraway*, the parents under state law were liable for the damage done to an old house by the teenagers ranging in age from 13 to 18. The defendants contended that the house was an attractive nuisance, as a defense. The court wrote that "appellants contend the house was in such a state of dilapidation the children were justified in thinking it an abandoned ghost house incapable of being damaged. That the juveniles may have considered the building a 'ghost house' or 'haunted house' is of no consequence inasmuch as the intention of a party committing vandalism does not affect the right of recovery of the injured party."

Product Liability and Halloween Costumes
Halloween Costumes --- what were they thinking?

In *Ferlito v. Johnson & Johnson*, Mrs. Ferlito had made costumes for a Halloween party in 1984 to depict her and her husband as Mary and her lamb. She made a lamb costume for Mr. Ferlito and she dressed as Mary. Mr. Ferlito's costume was made of long underwear with Johnson & Johnson cotton batting glued over the entire outfit including an elaborate headpiece "complete with ears." While at the party, Mr. Ferlito lit his butane lighter for a cigarette and his arm caught fire, eventually causing burns on one-third of his body. In testimony, both Mr. and Mrs. Ferlito testified that they knew that the cotton would burn, and that a warning of its flammability would not have changed their actions. The court found that since using the cotton batting in a costume was not a foreseeable use of the product, Johnson & Johnson had no duty to warn not to use the cotton batting on costumes.

The Ferlitos were awarded a total of $620,000 ($550,000 to Mr. Ferlito and $70,000 to Mrs. Ferlito) by a jury who found Johnson & Johnson and the Ferlito couple equally at fault. However, on appeal to the Sixth Circuit, U.S. Court of Appeals, the court found because the Ferlitos could not establish that a failure to warn was the proximate cause of their injuries that they could not establish a product liability tort under state law. Thus, the court refused to set aside a ruling which granted Johnson & Johnson a new trial. *Ferlito v. Johnson & Johnson*, 983 F.2d 1066 (6th Cir. 1992).

The Sixth Circuit court wrote that Ms. Ferlito was "Little Bo-Peep", but the U.S. District Court found that she was "Mary" while both agreed that Mr. Ferlito was a lamb. It is important to have reliable facts.

The court found that using cotton batting was not a foreseeable use of the product, so Johnson & Johnson had no duty to warn against it. However, this is not the first time that injuries have occurred as a result of making a costume with cotton balls, nor is it the last.

Halloween 2011, Kelly Boozan made a sheep costume from cotton balls which completely covered her body. While cooking on the stove, her costume ignited and her friends were able to put out the fire and rush her to the hospital where she sustained burns over one-third of her body.

One has to wonder if Johnson & Johnson still thinks making a costume from cotton balls is unforeseeable and they still have no duty to warn?

Sherri Perper, who lives in Oakland Gardens, New Jersey, filed a lawsuit in Queens County, New York again Forum Novelties in Melville, L.I., as well as Rubie's Costume Company and Party City for injuries she

64

sustained after falling in "clown shoes" she obtained from the defendant. She claimed that they were "dangerous" according to a New York Post newspaper account. This sounds like product liability which means that they claimed the product was defective in design which is the amusing irony of clown shoes! Defective in manufacture or defective in marketing might be other claims they might make. The outcome of the litigation is unknown.

Intentional torts
Assault

In the *Bouton* case discussed in Halloween Criminal Law, Bouton was acquitted of murder where he shot to death a 13-year-old boy with a plastic machine gun when he rang the doorbell on Halloween night. Here, again, are the facts from the case, *Bouton v. Allstate Insurance Co.*, 491 So.2d 56 (1st Cir. 1986):

This suit arose from the unfortunate events of Halloween night in 1981. Jeffrey Scott Trammel, aged 15, Robert Martin Landry, Jr., aged 13, and Daniel Breaux, aged 13, went trick-or-treating that evening. About 6:30 p.m., Trammel and Breaux rang Robert Bouton's (plaintiff) front door bell while Landry waited at the sidewalk. Plaintiff opened the door and saw Breaux standing before him. Breaux was dressed in military fatigues and was holding a plastic model submachine gun. Plaintiff shut the door immediately and locked it, then armed himself with a .357 magnum pistol. He returned to the door, opened it, and saw a flash of light, caused, he alleges, by Trammel's triggering a photographic flash. Plaintiff's pistol then discharged, the bullet striking and killing Breaux.

The case is not what you may be expecting. Bouton was indicted and tried for second-degree murder in Louisiana, but in this case he is suing the three boys (one of whom he shot to death) for causing him to be

65

arrested and defending himself for the murder. Why? Because they committed the intentional tort of assault by appearing at his door and threatening harm to him, he claimed.

The court applied the reasonableness test and held that a "reasonable person acting reasonably would not have been apprehensive of battery when confronted with 13-year-old boy, on Halloween, ringing the doorbell while dressed in fatigues and carrying plastic submachine gun."

You have completed the Halloween Tort Law course and now you know how Halloween costumes, haunted houses and trick or treat encounters can lead to litigation with grave consequences. Don't be negligent with your test taking and proceed to your Final Examination in Halloween Tort Law.

Final Examination 7. Halloween Tort Law

1.   Patrons of Haunted Houses accept that the owners and actors of the haunted house have a modified legal duty
A.   to take reasonable care.
B.   to warn.
C.   to protect.
D.   not to scare.

2.   Negligence cases also have to prove that the duty to protect is based on
A.   a foreseeable risk.
B.   a one in a million risk.
C.   a risk on Halloween only.
D.   anything that causes an injury

3.   Product liability for costumes could be based on
A.   defective design.
B.   defective manufacture.
C.   defective marketing.
D.   all of the above.

ANSWERS
Final Examination 7. Halloween Tort Law

1.   The answer is D.
The court has specifically described a modified duty "not to scare" in haunted houses, because that is what the patron is paying for. All of the other duties are the same in haunted houses.

2.   The answer is A.
To have a duty in negligence it must be for a foreseeable harm or risk. Choice B is a remote risk, choice C is a risk that is limited to Halloween, and choice D is too broad.

3.   The answer is D.
This one was the description of any product liability claim. While the "clown shoes case" may have confused you as to which theory they used for the claim that the clown shoes were dangerous, you are not alone.

Advanced Courses

All of these first year courses you have just experienced in the spirit of Halloween appear on state bar examinations and on the Multi-State Bar Examination (MBE) which has become a standard test for almost every state bar.

Once the first year courses have been completed and you have passed all of your examinations in each course, you are prepared to move on to the advanced law courses in law school.

Proceed, if you dare . . . .

Congratulations.

Moohahahaha.

❀❀❀❀❀
Halloween Employment Law

Employees can't resist wearing Halloween costumes to work, which often creates some unintended consequences. The costumes that are selected often reveal more about our co-workers than we really want to know, and sometimes bad judgment prevails.

Don't forget, sexual harassment is still sexual harassment, and a Halloween costume is not a defense.

Sexual harassment in the workplace is prohibited under Title VII of the 1964 Civil Rights Act, as amended, and through each state's laws. The definition of sexual harassment is "unwelcome verbal, visual, or physical conduct of a sexual nature that is severe or pervasive and affects working conditions or creates a hostile work environment."

Remember the Halloween Law principle that people do and say things they might not ordinarily do on any other day of the year. But to meet the definition of "hostile work environment" it typically takes a pattern of behaviors in the workplace. Halloween could simply add to a list of grievances about sexual harassment or be the final straw for someone who has felt sexually harassed.

What happens when a male supervisor reacts to a female employee's doctor costume in a way that is offensive in a sexual way to the female employee? In this Minnesota case, the Court of Appeals said that it was sexual harassment. In *Devane v. Sears Home Improvement Products, Inc.*, (Minn. Dec. 23, 2003), a sales employee filed a sexual harassment suit for, among other things, a manager who proceeded to unbuckle his belt and point to his groin area, saying "[H]ere Doctor. It hurts here." The Court of Appeals in Minnesota affirmed the state district court's ruling against the employer for

71

sexual harassment and hostile work environment claims.

Workers Compensation

Workers Compensation is a collective fund supported by the state and business taxes to cover employee injuries in the course of their employment. This helps reduce a major risk to businesses who might otherwise be faced with damage awards, leading to bankruptcy, ending the business and also failing to compensate the injured employee.

Halloween may invite the prankster problem in the workplace that represents another application of the Halloween Law principle: People do things on Halloween they might never do on any other day of the rest of the year. If it is a work day, then the possibilities are endless.

In 1950, Dora Kaplan who was employed by the sorority, Alpha Epsilon Phi, at the University of Minnesota, was injured when someone greased a streetside curb as a Halloween prank. She applied to the state Commission for compensation but she was denied payment. They said she was really on the way to Temple services and therefore was not on a journey where her work was the "dominant" purpose.

The court saw it differently and said the Commission had misapplied the dominant purpose test. Dora was first on her way to the drugstore to get some bandaids to replenish the supply in the sorority house that Halloween night, and afterward, she was continuing her journey to the Temple. The court remanded the case to the Commission to reapply the test and find that Dora should have been compensated. *Kaplan v. Alpha Epsilon Phi*, (Minn.,1950).

Some things never change, and in 1993 another workers compensation claim was made by an employee who was standing on a ladder when their co-worker frightened them with a mask, and they fell off the ladder,

72

injuring themselves. The only question to be resolved was the amount of the compensation. *Travis v. Robbins-Sykes Hardwood Flooring*, (Nov. 17, 1993).

Employees in Haunted Houses

The work in haunted houses can be particularly hazardous, and workers compensation must be paid if the injury occurs to an employee injured working in the scope of their duties.

In the next case, an employee was injured when he fell down an elevator shaft in a haunted house. The court captured the spirit of Halloween writing the opinion:

Haunted houses may be full of ghosts, goblins, and guillotines, but it's their more prosaic features that pose the real danger. Tyler Hodges found that out when an evening shift working the ticket booth ended with him plummeting down an elevator shaft. But as these things go, this case no longer involves Mr. Hodges. Years ago he recovered from his injuries, received a settlement, and moved on. This lingering specter of a lawsuit concerns only two insurance companies and who must foot the bill. And at the end of it all, we find, there is no escape for either of them.

The problems began at the front door of the Bricktown Haunted House in Oklahoma City. There Mr. Hodges was working the twilight hours checking tickets as guests entered. When the flashlight he used began flickering and then died, he ventured inside in search of a replacement. To navigate his way through the inky gloom, Mr. Hodges used the light of his cell phone. But when an actor complained that the light dampened the otherworldly atmosphere, Mr. Hodges turned it off and stumbled along as best he could. He was aiming for the freight elevator, where (imprudently, it turns out) spare flashlights were stored. When he reached the elevator, Mr. Hodges lifted the wooden gate across the entrance and stepped in. But because of the brooding darkness, Mr.

73

Hodges couldn't see that the elevator was on a floor above him and he crashed 20 feet down the empty elevator shaft. Western World Ins. Co. v. Markel American Ins. Co., (Okla.), 2012.

Is being an actor in a company haunted house within the scope of employment? It wasn't in the case of *Jordan v. Oakwood Homes*, 167 N.C. App.371,(2004), where an employee who was pretending to stab a co-worker followed by lunging at the crowd in a haunted house. She then fell from the table and injured her back. The company was found liable for the employees' injuries, and they were not covered by workers compensation insurance.

Another haunted house legal question arose about whether a workers compensation insurer had to defend its insured, Gardner, individually and doing business as Doc Fright, Haunted Philadelphia and Festival of Fears, aptly named.

There were two questions that had to be answered. (1) whether Samantha was an employee as defined by the policy; and (2) whether she was injured in the scope of her duties. The insurance company hoped to avoid the duty to defend Gardner, but the court found otherwise. The court found that Samantha had been "molested" by another employee, who had been hired by Gardner without checking and finding he had "violent propensities."

The first question was answered by determining whether Samantha was a seasonal employee. The court concluded that seasonal workers were temporary workers under the insurance policy, meaning "a person who is furnished to you to substitute for a permanent 'employee' on leave or to meet seasonal or short term workload conditions." Thus, the court determined that any employee hired 14 days before Halloween was a seasonal employee.

Secondly, the court had to determine if Samantha's injury occurred during the course of her employment. To do this, the court used the "but for" test to find that "but for" Samantha's employment by Gardner, she would not have been molested, since the attack occurred during the time of their employment on the premises of the Festival of Fears. *Nautilus v. Gardner* (E.D.Pa. 2005).

Doc Fright, Festival of Fears and Haunted Philadelphia had failed to protect Samantha, its minor employee, but won the right to be defended by its insurer, Nautilus.

In 2011, it was reported that a 17-year-old employee was found unconscious, hanging in a noose-prop in Creepyworld, a haunted house in Fenton, Missouri. It was reported as an apparent accident slip from a bathtub where she had climbed and put her head in the noose. If the employee qualified as an employee and was acting within the scope of her duties (acting as someone hanging from a noose?) then just as in the *Nautilus* case, the insurer would be required to defend Creepyworld. A settlement would prevent this civil case from going to trial.

Religion, Employers and Halloween

Some religions do not permit participation in the celebration of Halloween and the Jehovah's Witness denomination is one of them. When an emergency medical technician was required by her work to attend a Halloween celebration at the local shopping mall, she refused, citing her religious objection. She was then dismissed from her job. The court sided with the employee and said that the employer had to make reasonable accommodation for her religious beliefs. *Equal Employment Opportunity Commission v. Community Transport Services*, LLC, Complaint, United States District Court, South Carolina, (Date Filed 09/10/09). The company failed to show at the court hearing and the judgment was entered for $33,435.02 in the employee's favor.

Final Examination 8. Halloween Employment Law

1.   If an employee arrives at her workplace, dressed in a Halloween costume as a cave woman, it is illegal if:

A.   Her male co-worker says, "Hey I'd like to drag you by the hair into MY cave," and he slaps her on her derriere.

B.   Her male co-worker says, "Hey I'd like to drag you by the hair into MY cave," and tries to drag her by the hair. A third co-worker points out, "She asked for it."

C.   Her male co-worker says, "Hey I'd like to drag you by the hair into MY cave," and pantomimes dragging her back to his cave, but doesn't touch her.

D.   A, B and C are legal if the woman does not find it to be "unwelcome," but welcomes the responses. A, B or C could be illegal if she considered them "unwelcome" responses.

2.   A permanent employee who manages the Haunted House entertainment center drives his car to pick up an order of bat wings for a Haunted House event, but before he returns to the Haunted House, he trades in his car and buys a new one. On the drive back to the Haunted House another driver runs into his car and he is injured.

Can the employee collect workers compensation?

A.   No. He cannot collect workers compensation because his primary purpose for the trip when he was injured was to trade his car.

B.   No. He cannot collect workers compensation because he was injured off the premises of the Haunted House.

C.   Yes, He can collect workers compensation because driving to pick up the bat wings for a job related purpose was the primary purpose of his trip.

D.   Yes. He can collect workers compensation because the accident causing his injury was not his fault.

3.   You are an employer and you have decided that you can avoid some of the legal pitfalls by requiring everyone to wear a costume, so no one feels left out. They will be fired if they don't. Is this an advisable strategy?

A.   No. It's Halloween and something will go wrong, anyway, so don't even try.
B.   No. Any costume in the workplace is illegal.
C.   No. Requiring an employee to celebrate Halloween if they object for a religious reason is not a reasonable accommodation.
D.   Yes. Who doesn't like celebrating Halloween?

ANSWERS

Final Examination 8. Halloween Employment Law

1.   The answer is D.

The definition of sexual harassment can involve verbal or physical or even a workplace hostile environment from a combination of more subtle sexual innuendo, but the key is that it has to be "unwelcome". So A, B or C could each be illegal under federal law but only if the employee finds the action to be "unwelcome."

Because the employer can be liable for the actions of workers who make unwelcome remarks of a sexual nature, many businesses prohibit the wearing of Halloween costumes at work.

2.   The answer is A.

The primary purpose of his trip was to trade his car, not to buy bat wings, and it would be extremely difficult to convince the court that the primary purpose of the trip was to pick up a bat wings for an event, when buying a car was at stake on the trip, thus choice C is incorrect. Choice B does not matter because a trip on behalf of the employer in the scope of one's duties does not require the employee to stay on the premises. Choice D would not matter in workers compensation as long as the primary purpose of the trip was in the scope of duties for the employee.

3.   The answer is C.

Requiring employees to wear a costume or be fired (particularly if they object for religious reasons) is a bad strategy because federal law, Title VII, requires employers to make reasonable accommodations for religious reasons of employees. Choice A may be true, but it is not the best answer. Choice B is just wrong. Choice D is what went wrong with this employer's strategy in the first place! Obviously, everyone does not enjoy celebrating Halloween if their religion to which they adhere prohibits it.

9

❋❋❋❋❋
Halloween Oil and Gas Law

Fracking in the cemetery is not a new song title, but it is the subject of a recent offer to a cemetery in Ohio for their mineral rights under the 75,000 dead bodies that are laid to rest there. But can they sell it? What do they have left to sell after they have sold the plot of land for someone's loved one to be laid to rest in peace forever?

One of the first principles taught in property law is the metaphor of the bundle of sticks. Property possession or ownership is made up of rights which can be likened to a bundle of sticks. In some bundles you have ownership, mineral rights, and rights to build a skyscraper; whereas in other bundles you have only the right to possess the property for a limited period of time, as in a lease. So property possession and ownership can be different depending upon the "sticks" in the deed and covenants.

So when you buy a plot in a cemetery, what kind of sticks do you have in your bundle? Certainly there is a kind of possession for a very long time --- some might wish for perpetuity, but is that possible? What kind of sticks are in the bundle? Who owns the mineral rights? Mineral rights include oil, gas, rock and other resources under the ground. Can you drill for oil on your plot? The answer, as you might imagine, is no. The owner of a plot has little more than a license or an easement, which may carry stipulations like whether the person being buried is a member of the church, if it is a church owned cemetery. So as a general rule for cemetery plots, there is no title which passes to the plot owner, only the limited right to bury there, and that may also be limited.

An easement is a non-possessory interest in another's property for limited use and enjoyment. The property owner is then limited in the way that the

79

property can be used because of that easement. Easements can be for underground pipelines, sidewalks along a private residential property or stringing overhead powerlines across a property. But there is no possession and there may be a restriction on transferring that right.

A license is also a non-possessory interest in land that is a personal grant of a right, which would limit the transfer of the interest.

So, none of the plot holders are going to get a windfall of oil profits.

But the title holders of the cemetery property are in Ohio are facing a different question. With an offer from an energy company to buy the mineral rights to utilize fracturing oil shale to recover valuable oil, it is a lucrative possibility. But would that disturb the easement given to bury the dead to rest in peace?

If fracking the oil shale underneath the bodies will disturb the bodies, then the title holders will likely violate their easement or license to the plot owner. But if the disturbance is only psychological to the survivors, it probably will not be quantifiable damages in any state.

In order to avoid violating the license or easement, the titleholder will need to do the best they can to avoid disturbing the plots, which would involve entering the underground at a good distance from the surface area, and having some assurances that the surface will not shift or collapse.

Questions of ownership of mineral rights are in the area of oil and gas law (a subject that is covered in some state bar examinations).

––––––––––––

It's time to gather your bundle of sticks and take the Halloween Oil and Gas Final Examination.

Final Examination 9. Halloween Oil and Gas Law

1. Does the right to drill for oil come with the plot your family bought from a cemetery corporation?

   ___yes   ___no

2. Do the vampires in a cemetery have a possessory interest in the plot in which they sleep?

   ___yes   ___no

3. If geothermal energy resources are discovered under a cemetery, can they be sold by the titleholder?

   ___yes   ___no

ANSWERS

Final Examination 9. Halloween Oil and Gas Law

1.   The answer is No.

A plot holder does not possess anything, so you have nothing to sell or license to an oil drilling company. Plots are either licenses or easements, for the most part. Note that the question refers to a cemetery corporation, which would hold the title. If it is a family cemetery, the ownership of the title might be shared by the plot owners, and then they would have a possessory interest.

2.   The answer is No.

That hot-looking vampire is just a renter, not a homeowner.

3.   The answer is Yes.

Geothermal energy resources are considered mineral rights and can be sold separately from the surface rights, just as oil and gas mineral rights. Geothermal energy is a bit more hellish and appropriate for Halloween, but so far, no cases have come up with a question of mining for geothermal energy under a cemetery. But "rest" assured, they would be handled the same way as oil and gas.

⚉⚉⚉⚉⚉

Halloween State and Local Government Law

Local ordinances have been passed specifically for the holiday of Halloween in New York City and Washington, D.C. which is a good indication that Halloween is a unique holiday. In order to enjoy the holiday, it requires enforcement of our social contract to give up a little freedom in exchange for regulating behavior that might be dangerous to civil society.

Government was created in order to enforce this social contract. Rousseau the philosopher of the 1700s established our concept of natural law and the freedoms that are natural. He described the social contract where we agree to forgo total lawlessness and instead pay taxes, and limit our freedoms in showing restraint in physical actions against others and even restraint in some speech. This we do in exchange for protection against crime, tainted food and invasion by foreign forces.

Local government has been granted the power by the state to pass laws which are best created and enforced at the local level. What better time to govern locally than Halloween?

It should also be noted that the Bill of Rights protections of individual freedoms are also held against local government. That is, local government must also restrain its actions from infringing on civil liberties. While it is clear that the Bill of Rights reads "Congress", it is generally agreed that the U.S. Supreme Court decided in the 1800s that all of the rights in the Bill of Rights were incorporated to the states through the other Amendments, thus any government "shall make no law . . . abridging the freedom of speech. . ." This freedom of speech also includes freedom of expression, including other forms of communication beyond speech. This might include costumes, yard displays, theatrical presentations, t-shirt slogans, badges with slogans, etc.

I want to express myself with my Halloween costume!

When local government tries to restrict expressing oneself with a costume, there must be some rational relationship to a legitimate purpose of government, such as for health and safety reasons to legally infringe on your Constitutional right of expression. For example, here are a few restrictions on disguises that have been passed by local governments which probably do not become real conflicts until Halloween:

In Alabama, using "garb or outward array" to pretend to be a clergyman, rabbi, nun or priest is a criminal misdeameanor and could mean jail time. However, the law requires "fraudulently pretending to be a clergyman." So as long as the wearer does nothing that meets the definition of fraud in Alabama while wearing such a costume, the wearer may escape falling within the intended net of this law.

Here's the Alabama statute:

Alabama.

Section 13A-14-4

Fraudulently pretending to be clergyman.

Whoever, being in a public place, fraudulently pretends by garb or outward array to be a minister of any religion, or nun, priest, rabbi or other member of the clergy, is guilty of a misdemeanor and, upon conviction, shall be punished by a fine not exceeding $500.00 or confinement in the county jail for not more than one year, or by both such fine and imprisonment. (Acts 1965, 1st Ex. Sess., No. 273, p. 381; Code 1975, §13-4-99.)

Some jurisdictions have passed ordinances prohibiting the wearing of "masks or disguises" in public places, such as this local ordinance in Walnut Creek, California:

84

17-32 Mask or disguise–Wearing.
No person shall wear a mask or disguise on a public
street without a permit from the sheriff.
(Code 1959, 4237.2) Walnut Creek, CA
Fortunately, legislators in Louisiana had the foresight to exempt the day of Halloween in their statute against the wearing of masks in public. [LSA-R.S. 14:313].

I want to express myself with Silly String art on Halloween! Is it art or is it litter?

Hollywood, CA   Photo used with
permission from Alan Pavilik

Hollywood could argue that they have a rational relationship between restricting your "Silly string" and the costs to taxpayers to clean it up the day after Halloween. If "Silly String" is litter, then the government need only have a rational relationship with the law and the legitimate purpose of clean streets. But if we see "Silly String" as expression, even an artistic expression, then the standard may change to a much higher one of a "compelling government purpose". If we accept that keeping the city clean is a compelling government purpose, then city officials must also ensure that they have met another of the requirements of infringing on a Constitutional right and that is to make it as narrow as possible so there are no overly broad regulations restricting activities that should not be infringed. By restricting it to the specific hours of Halloween, the local government has "narrowly tailored" its infringing regulation sufficiently to probably pass Constitutional muster.

So is "Silly String" on Halloween litter or is it art? It's Hollywood, so I'm going with "art"!

How can my local government change the day for Halloween or restricting the age for trick-or-treating?

When local governments regulate based on children's ages, it is usually about the *parens patriae* role of government in protecting society's children. *Parens patriae* is the latin term for "parent of the nation" meaning that the state has a duty to act as a parent when there are risks in society that would warrant protection of children. For example, drinking age, and X-rated movies which are used to restrict certain ages from attending are examples of those kinds of laws which are Constitutional infringements on kids' freedoms.

Connecticut's legislature has proposed changing the date of Halloween within its jurisdiction, claiming a positive effect on public safety for children, less harried parents and a boost to the economy. But remember, the standard is pretty low for passing a law that does not involve a constitutionally protected right. The standard is simply whether the law has a "rational relationship" to a legitimate government purpose you are trying to achieve. If you can scare up even a little rationality in its logic, it is probably enough to be a constitutionally valid law.

Here's the news from The Hartford Currant:

State Lawmaker Wants to Change the Date of Halloween to Ensure it Always Falls on a Saturday

October 24, 2011 | By DANIELA ALTIMARI

HARTFORD — Everyone knows Halloween in celebrated on Oct. 31 but a state lawmaker wants to tamper with tradition to ensure the holiday is always marked on a weekend.

State Rep. Tim Larson is proposing that the legislature designate the last Saturday in October as Halloween. He says it would make the holiday less harried for working parents, safer for trick-or-treaters and boost the economy as well.

One would have to believe that Halloween had gotten a bit out of hand in Rehoboth Beach, Delaware when you read their ordinance. They have the most complicated of all the Halloween control ordinances for the celebration of the holiday. They have carved out an exception for going about the streets and sidewalks on Halloween for those younger than 14 years old. They also regulated when "treats" would take place on Halloween, should it fall on a Sunday. There is even a part B. Part B provides an exception for the Rehoboth Beach Chamber of Commerce or service clubs who might wish to have Halloween parties or parades.

198-33. Halloween regulations; exceptions. [Amended 10-14-1977 by Ord. No. 1077-2; 10-11-1991 by Ord. No. 1091-1]

A.No person shall permit his child or any child under his control to go about the streets, ways and/or sidewalks within the corporate limits of the City of Rehoboth Beach for the purpose of causing mischief of any sort; provided, however, that children who have not

87

attained the age of 14 years may go upon the streets, ways and/or sidewalks from door to door or house to house for treats between the hours of 6:00 p.m., prevailing time, and 8:00 p.m., prevailing time, on October 31 of any year; provided, however, that if October 31 shall be a Sunday, such going from door to door and house to house for treats shall take place on the evening of October 30 between the hours of 6:00 p.m., prevailing time, and 8:00 p.m., prevailing time.

B. Nothing in this section shall be deemed to prohibit the gathering and participation of children in a Halloween parade or costume contest sponsored by the Rehoboth Beach Chamber of Commerce or the service clubs of the city.

In Bellville, Missouri, a local ordinance prohibits trick-or-treaters past the eighth grade. In an interview with the St. Louis Post Dispatch, the Mayor was quoted as saying, *"We believe that Halloween is for little children"*

If the mayor is having the effect of restricting the individual freedom of adults, many of whom are not bank robbers in masks using Halloween as a cover for their crime, perhaps the local government has been a bit too broad with their regulation. But if a ninth grader asking for candy going door to door does not rise to a constitutionally protected right, then the local government probably has met the lower standard of a rational relationship to public safety of the homeowners.

Maybe you were thinking that this might be an infringement on another First Amendment constitutional right, the right to association? According to the U.S. Supreme Court, there is no right to association between, for example, eighth graders and ninth graders. In *Dallas v. Stanglin*, 490 U.S. 19 (1989) the court upheld a Dallas ordinance that restricted a teenage dance hall to ages 14 to 18. Halloween is but one day a year and does not come with any special rights of association, so the Mayor of Bellville can breathe a sigh of relief for Halloween and the threat of those ninth graders.

Don't Let your Boys Grow up to be Cowboys

This course on Halloween State and Local Government Law would not be complete without this 1930s case from the Wild West. Some boys were "engaged in performing a series of disturbances known as Halloween pranks, and that they consisted of riding horseback on the sidewalk, pushing wagon wheels over a beet dump, making loud and tumultuous noises and commotion throughout the evening." The Deputy Sheriff had grown impatient with their antics and ran after the boys as they were pushing a tank wagon down the street, demanding that they stop. When they didn't stop he fired two shots from his pistol and seriously injured one of the boys with one of his shots. "Hatfield testified, among other things, that he was trying to keep the boys from 'getting into anything,' and in answer to a question proposed by plaintiffs' counsel, 'Just what was your idea in shooting?' he answered, 'To make him know some one had authority to stop him.'"

The court did not find that his reason mattered, and while the court found they had violated the specific statute that prohibits damaging wagons and assembling to cause mischief, they still held that the deputy sheriff had acted unlawfully. *Corder v. People*, 87 Colo. 251, 287 (Colo. 1930).

❀❀❀❀❀

You are ready to take the State and Local Government Final Examination, and you have probably found that Halloween happens at the local level, so it is not surprising to find Halloween State and Local Government Law an important advanced course in Halloween Law.

Final Examination 10. Halloween State and Local Government Law

1. State and local governments have power to pass criminal laws to protect their citizens at the local level.

_____yes   _____no

2. State and local government can infringe the Constitutional freedoms of children on Halloween when they could not otherwise infringe those of adults, based on what power?

A.   Children are messy and need to be regulated.

B.   Hansel and Gretel visited the Gingerbread House with criminal consequences and should be a lesson to any children visiting houses on Halloween. Thus, it is a power to regulate kids.

C.   Children on Halloween are engaged in activities which are potentially dangerous, including walking in the dark and possibly visiting strangers' houses.

D.   State and local government have the power to regulate based on *parens patriae* principle that the government acts as the parent to protect against societal risks to children.

3.   My right of expression is infringed when local government restricts the kind of costume that I can wear. How can they do that?

A.   Rousseau's social contract of law requires that you tolerate some infringement on your liberties to protect society as a whole, like those who would use Halloween to rob a bank and not be noticed in a mask.

B.   Government can infringe freedoms when there is a compelling government interest like public safety.

C.   Government can infringe freedoms when it is narrowly tailored and not overly broad.

D.   All of the above.

90

ANSWERS

Final Examination 10. Halloween State and Local Government Law

1. The answer is "yes".
Local governments derive their power from the sovereignty of the state government and the delegation of that power to local governments. Protecting citizens from crime is a basic function of government in carrying out their social contract. If you missed this, then go back and read about Rousseau until you are convinced.

2. The answer is D.
You might have thought the answer was C, but the question was about what power, rather than the rational relationship test. Yes, a bit of a trick question, but you are saavy Halloween law students at this point. Some may have picked the answer with the latin in it --- always a good choice in answering a question about law. Choice B is not correct, although a local government might try it. Choice A is simply a matter of opinion, and may be most applicable to Halloween, but it is not a power.

3. The answer is D.
A, B and C are all correct, which means there is a lot that goes into infringing an individual liberty if a local or state government does so.

11

Halloween Education Law

Schools that engage in activities around Halloween have the same legal obligations the rest of the year. The principle of Halloween, that people do things around Halloween that they wouldn't do any other time of the year, also applies to schools and school districts.

Schools are a place where conflict about whether Halloween should be celebrated also occurs. The Associated Press reported that the Springfield School District through Superintendent Michael Davino had "barred" elementary school children from wearing costumes on Halloween. After parents protested, the policy was withdrawn citing parties that were already planned (a good enough reason).

Recalling Halloween Constitutional Law and the *Guyer* case in the Establishment Clause discussion, the school district had been sued by a parent because they were celebrating Halloween and allowing the students to dress in costumes. The court had to determine if this was a government entanglement in religion, presumptively vacraft-type religion. It is worth repeating the court's conclusion here, in Halloween Education Law:

The court held that the mere depiction of witches, cauldrons and brooms, and related costumes, in context of public elementary school's Halloween celebration did not have primary effect of endorsing or promoting religion and, thus, did not violate establishment clause even assuming such symbols could have religious significance to followers of particular religion related to witchcraft; no religious ceremony was alleged to have occurred, and decorations served secular purpose of enriching children's educational background, cultural awareness, and sense of community.

Injuries at School Halloween Activities?

Not a question of if, but when and how much. The school district owes a duty to protect the children in its care during the time that the children are there. To be liable for negligence, the school district would have to breach that duty. A defense might be that there was "assumption of the risk" by the student (and their parents), for example when a student joins the wrestling team or football team. But that assumption is for specific risks like injuries related to those sports, not the risk of being molested by the coach, for example.

A teacher in Taunton, Massachusetts, thought it would be funny to "scare" students by coming to the classroom door dressed in a mask and brandishing a chainsaw. Unfortunately, the 15-year-old student who answered the door was frightened, and tripped over a chair while trying to run away. The fall resulted in a fractured bone and serious knee injury that required surgery. The student, who was on crutches for months, had to give up playing sports.

The family of the boy sought $100,000 in compensation for medical expenses. It is unknown what came of the demand letter that was sent to the school district, but presumably there was a settlement.

In *Drake*, a school district was held liable when a student who was preparing a silo for a haunted house became ill from *histoplasmosis*, a bird dropping disease, from the presence of bird droppings in the silo. While the administrator was aware of the danger of *histoplasmosis* and warned the owner of the silo to clean it before the students entered it, it was clear that the injury was foreseeable. But most importantly, the court found that as a result of knowing of the danger, as a school they had a duty to warn the students about the danger of *histoplasmosis*, which they failed to do. The case before the court was whether to reverse the dismissal of the case against the School district. The court did reverse, based on the breach of the duty to warn. The immunity of the school was not sufficient to protect the school from the legal duty to warn.

Final Examination 11. Halloween Education Law

1.   Can the school district ban Halloween parties in all the elementary schools?
          ____Yes   ____No

2.   Does a school district have a duty to keep students safe in school related activities, even those for Halloween?
          ____Yes   ____No

3.   Did it make a difference that the administrator in the Drake case was aware of the dangers of *histoplasmosis* in the silo, where the students were sickened from the bird droppings in the silo while preparing it as a haunted house?

          ____Yes   ____No

ANSWERS
Final Examination 11. Halloween Education Law

1.   The answer is Yes.

The school district has the power to regulate as long as they are not entangled with a religious reason (infringement on the Establishment Clause) or directing the regulation specifically to ban a religion (Free Exercise Clause). But they will have to incur the wave of unhappy children and parents which may be a suitable reason not to ban Halloween activities. On the other hand, some schools have had parents demand that they not involve their children in Halloween. In that case, the school can make reasonable accommodations for that child not to participate.

2.   The answer is Yes.

The school does not get a free pass for Halloween. There are no modified duties even the duty "not to scare" for administrators if the scaring results in an injury as in the case in Taunton, Massachusetts.

3.   The answer is Yes.

In *Drake*, the school administrator knew of the risk os *histoplasmosi*s because they had been introduced to the disease before. They advised exercising caution with entering the silo before the bird droppings were cleaned. However, the students jumped the gun and started work in the silo before the droppings were removed and so they were exposed. Despite the effort to address the disease, the plan was not supervised and the students were injured. Because the administrator was aware of the danger, unforeseeability was not a defense for the school district. (See the chapter on Halloween Tort Law.)

❀❀❀❀❀

🎃🎃🎃🎃🎃
Halloween Legal Ethics

Nothing on Earth is so beautiful as the final haul on Halloween night. ---Stephen Almond

All lawyers who have passed the Bar Examination and are members with their respective state bar associations are bound by their respective state ethics regulations. These regulations are based on the American Bar Association Model Rules of Professional Conduct.

The number one rule, literally, is regarding competence and the client-lawyer relationship:

Client-Lawyer Relationship
Rule 1.1 Competence

A lawyer shall provide competent representation to a client. Competent representation requires the legal knowledge, skill, thoroughness and preparation reasonably necessary for the representation.

During the mortgage foreclosure period, law firms for banks and lending institutions may have been tempted to do "robo-signing," or signing mortgage foreclosures without really verifying the facts. This is considered a violation of legal ethics.

The Steven J. Baum, P.C. law firm in suburban Buffalo was one of the largest foreclosure firms in New York in terms of volume of mortgages foreclosed, according to the New York Law Journal (Feb. 2010). In keeping with the principle that Halloween parties may be places where people do things they would not otherwise do the rest of the year, the Steven J. Baum company was a glowing example of this principle. But should that be a defense?

The Halloween party for the firm in 2010 was on the theme of foreclosure and the staff and attorneys dressed as homeless people who had been foreclosed on by the firm. Besides showing insensitivity and bad judgment, the firm's business practices raised state ethics law questions about their behavior the rest of the year. New York Attorney General Eric Schneiderman investigated the firm's practices and in March 2012 reached a settlement agreement with the firm in the amount of $4 million. According to the New York Law Journal, the attorney general's office press release on March 22, 2012 found that "the Baum firm 'repeatedly' filed legal papers in foreclosure and bankruptcy proceedings 'without taking appropriate steps to verify the accuracy of' allegations, the lender's right to foreclose or to file a bankruptcy proof of claim." The settlement includes resolution of allegations that the Baum Firm, Pillar, Steven J. Baum, and Kumiega violated New York Executive Law § 63(12) and General Business Law § 349, although they continue to deny any wrongdoing. In an ironic twist, the firm closed its doors in 2011 after the news broke.

A former employee sent photos of the Halloween party to reporter Joe Nocera of *The New York Times*, and they were published October 28, 2011. The article started a collective outrage against the firm, which preceded the closing of the Steven J. Baum Firm. Photo from *The New York Times*, Oct. 29, 2012.

With all of these conflicts on Halloween, wouldn't you expect lawyers to be specializing in cases to litigate? If you said "yes" to that question, you would be right. One firm has an advertisement specifically targeting anyone who has suffered a personal injury due to Halloween activities.

The Schmidt and Clark law firm website text gives you all you need to know to find a lawyer who wants to talk to you about your Halloween injury lawsuit.

Do I have a Halloween Injury Lawsuit?
The Personal Injury & Product Liability Litigation Group at our law firm is an experienced team of trial lawyers that focus on the representation of plaintiffs in Halloween injury accident lawsuits. We are handling individual litigation nationwide and currently accepting new cases in all 50 states.
Free Halloween Injury Case Evaluation: Has your child or other loved one sustained an injury on someone's property or been injured by a defective Halloween costume or product? If so, you should contact our law firm immediately. You may be entitled to compensation by filing a lawsuit and we can help.

Attention Attorneys: *Schmidt & Clark considers a referral from another law firm to be one of the greatest compliments. Our law firm has built a reputation for success and accepts a number of case referrals on a regular basis. We do not publish prior verdicts or settlements on our website. If you would like to refer us a case or for us to send you a profile of prior award judgments or average referral fees, please visit the attorney referral section of our website.*

http://www.schmidtandclark.com/halloween-injury-lawyer-lawsuit

---

Advertising by lawyers is perfectly legal. Soliciting people who have specific injuries is perfectly ethical. But timing is everything. There are times when soliciting clients is not legal. For example, in a case in Florida, *Florida Bar v. Went For It, Inc.* in 1995, the U.S. Supreme Court ruled that lawyers could not solicit by direct mail, families of car accident or disaster victims in less than 30 days from the date of the accident. The reason? Justice O'Connor wrote that the limitation on solicitation served the important goal of "protecting the privacy and tranquility of personal injury victims and their loved ones against intrusive unsolicited contact by lawyers." While this rule applies to Florida, almost every state has a similar restriction on solicitation of clients.

That goes for Halloween injury victims, too.

You are ready to go on to your Legal Ethics in Halloween Law final examination. Really, it's not scary. And remember, no cheating!

Final Examination 12. Halloween Legal Ethics Law

1. Why did Stephen J. Baum have to pay $4 million in fines to the state of New York?

A.   He violated the New York Business Code.
B.   He was insensitive to the people he evicted.
C.   He bought a big house with his profits.
D.   He violated the New York Legal Ethics Code.

2. Should I go to an attorney who advertises for clients who have been injured due to faulty Halloween products?

A.   Yes. In general, advertising for lawyers is completely ethical.
B.   Yes. In general, advertising for lawyers is unethical and I am looking for an unethical lawyer.
C.   No. All advertising by lawyers is distasteful and unethical.
D.   No. If the lawyer is in Florida and contacts you directly with a solicitation in less than 30 days of the incident or accident, that would be a violation of the Florida state ethics code.

ANSWERS
Final Examination 12. Halloween Legal Ethics

1.   The answer is A.

While all of these answers are true, only A is the correct answer as to why Baum had to pay $4 million. B is certainly true in that he was insensitive to the people he evicted and C is certainly true that he bought a big house, but none of these things are unethical.

It is unclear if any finding was made about violating legal ethics. The Attorney General's settlement agreement restricted Baum and his partner to suspend their representation of mortgage clients for two years. So Baum and his partner could open up another kind of practice, for example a personal injury practice for people who have been injured by Halloween costumes. He has some personal experience with that one, too.

2. The answer is D.

Answer A is clearly wrong, because only certain circumstances make advertising unethical for lawyers. Answer B is wrong because A is wrong, but beyond that an unethical lawyer is someone to avoid. How can you trust an unethical lawyer? You need to be able to trust your lawyer on some level, and an unethical lawyer should not be trusted on any level. Answer C is thought to be true by many in the profession who find advertising to be distasteful and unethical, but that does not make it unethical in the state legal ethics code.

Answer D, is the right answer in every way, based on the Florida case, *Florida Bar v. Went For It, Inc.*

———————

Congratulations on passing your Legal Ethics Examination (without cheating of course). If you go on to graduate from law school and intend to practice law, you will also need to take a special exam on legal ethics. Yes, legal ethics has become so important to the profession that a separate examination is required in almost every state called the MPRE (Multi-State Professional Ethics examination), and can be taken while you are still in law school.

13
Omitted

This is Halloween Law, and there will be no chapter 13.

Since Friday, October 13, 1307 when King Philip IV of France arrested (and murdered) the Knights Templar, Friday the 13th has been considered an unlucky day. It certainly was for the Knights Templar.

Some buildings leave out the 13th floor, and some airlines omit row 13 on their aircraft.

So in the spirit of Halloween, the superstitious and those who suffer from triskaidekaphobia (fear of the number thirteen), Halloween Law will omit chapter thirteen.

14

✿✿✿✿✿
Halloween Military Law

Members of the military are regulated under the Uniform Code of Military Justice, with a system of trial courts and appeals courts separate from those of civilians for conduct within the course of their military service.

One of the important codes of conduct that is important to Halloween Law is "conduct unbecoming an officer and a gentleman" (8 specifications), in violation of Article 133, Uniform Code of Military Justice, 10 USC § 933. Halloween can mean the difference between staying in the service with honor or being dishonorably discharged. *U.S. v. Modesto,* Court of Appeals for the Armed Forces, (Sept 29, 1995).

The case started out with a rather simple charge of "conduct unbecoming an officer and a gentleman" against Col. Modesto for an ample range of conduct beginning with his identification in a number of indecent-exposure incidents where the perpetrator was a male dressed as a woman. This investigation led to the discovery of his performance as a female impersonator at a gay club, and photographs "and other evidence seized in a lawful search of appellant's off-post home [which] unequivocally proved his participation in conduct unbecoming an officer including sodomy, mutual masturbation, indecent touching of another male, cross-dressing in public, performing as a female impersonator in a night club, and imitating fellatio with two other men."

Col. Modesto was convicted but his defense counsel tried to raise the question of whether other men in the Army also cross-dressed from time to time, which led to an appeal when it was discovered that one of the male members of the court --- a Brigadier General --- had once dressed as a woman in North Korea.

At the appeal, it was made very clear that the Brigadier General had dressed as a woman at a Halloween party, thus making it perfectly acceptable and not at all unbecoming of an officer and a gentleman. The court made two distinctions. First, the Brigadier General's costume was worn at a Halloween party, and was therefore "innocuous personal behavior similar to the cross-dressing in a King Neptune ceremony that this Court stated was not prejudicial to good order and discipline"; and second, the Brigadier General "was not presenting himself as a woman but, rather, was in female attire at a function recognized as a costume party."

So in the end, the court held that there was no reason that the Brigadier General should have been excluded from the court because of this previous event when he dressed as a woman at a Halloween party, nor was there any prejudice from him because of this background.

The distinction? A Halloween party.

Final Examination 14. Halloween Military Law

1. The military are subject to the Uniform Military Code of Justice and are tried in a military court system completely separate from the civilian system.

____true   ____false

2. The military law which requires officers to abstain from "conduct unbecoming an officer and a gentleman" is distinguishable based on whether it was at a Halloween party, at least in *United States v. Modesto*?

____yes, absolutely, in part   ___no, positively, in part

ANSWERS
Final Examination 14. Halloween Military Law

1. True. This one is fairly straightforward if you read the title to this chapter, but you get full credit for getting it right, anyway.

2. Yes, positively, in part. The use of the word, "in part" is also a good lawyer term when talking about court opinions. Remember to use it. You can almost always find something to talk about "in part" because the court almost always rules on more than one legal issue. Especially in an appeals case, there may be positive and negative holdings. In this case, the part where the court had ruled on the "conduct unbecoming an officer and a gentleman" was at least, *in part*, distinguished by the fact that one event was at a Halloween party. Of course, another part of the conviction was based on identifying Col. Modesto as the perpetrator in several indecent-exposure cases which was completely separate from the other issues.

Congratulations. You have passed Military Law which you can see is essential in Halloween Law.

15

⬤⬤⬤⬤⬤

Halloween Law and You

Congratulations!

You have successfully completed your study of Halloween Law.

So the real test of your knowledge of Halloween Law is just beginning. Now you will need to try out your new skills during the Halloween season, and particularly on the day of Halloween. Remember the first scary principle of Halloween Law – people do and say things they would never do on any other day of the year.

Now you may go to the end of the book for evidence of your completion of Halloween Law, suitable for framing --- if you dare!

Moooooohahahahaha.

List of Cases

Arthur v. City of DeRidder, 799 So. 2d 589 (La.App. 3rd Cir.2001).

Atkinson v. State, 58 Neb. 356, 78 N.W. 621 (Neb. 1899).

Bonanno v. Continental Casualty Co., 285 So.2d 591 (La.App. 4th Cir.1973).

Bouton v. Allstate Ins. Co., 491 So. 2d 56, 59 (La. Ct. App. 1986).

Burton v. Carroll Cnty., 60 S.W.3d 829 (Tenn. Ct. App. 2001).

Cantu Herrera v. Dretke, F.Supp.2d (not reported), 2004 WL 3331891 (S.D.Tex.,2004).

Central Virginia Community College v. Katz, 546 U.S. 356 (2006).

Chaplinsky v. New Hampshire, 315 U.S. 568 (1942).

Cohen v. California, 403 U.S. 15, 20, 91 S.Ct. 1780, 29 L.Ed.2d 284 (1971).

Com. v. Riva, 18 Mass.App.Ct. 713, 469 N.E.2d 1307, Mass.App.,1984.

Dallas v. Stanglin, 490 U.S. 19 (1989).

Daniels v. Manhattan and Bronx Surface Transit Operating Authority, 1999 WL 276226 (1st Dep't).

Devane v. Sears Home Improvement Products, Inc., 2003 Minn. App. LEXIS 1514 (Minn. Dec. 23, 2003).

Doe v. Nixon, No. 4:08-cv-1518-CEJ, 2009 WL 2957925 (E.D.Mo.) aff'd (Mo., 2008).

Drake by Drake v. Mitchell Community Schools, 628 N.E.2d 1231, Ind.App. 1 Dist.,1994 (February 02, 1994).

Durmon v. Billings. 873 So. 2d 872 (La. Ct. App. 2004).

Ferlito v. Johnson & Johnson, 983 F.2d 1066 (6th Cir. 1992).

Ferlito v. Johnson & Johnson,771 F. Supp. 196 ((E.D.Mich. 1991).

Florida Bar v. Went For It, Inc., 115 S.Ct. 2371, 132 L. Ed. 2d 541 (1995).

Fox v. Doe, 12 Misc.3d 1168(A), 820 N.Y.S.2d 842 (2006).

Friends of Temescal Canyon, Inc. v. City of Los Angeles, Not Reported in Cal.Rptr.3d, 2005 WL 1524201, Cal.App. 2 Dist. (June 29, 2005).

Galan v. Covenant House of New Orleans, 96-1006 (La.App. 5th Cir.5/14/97), 695 So.2d 1007 (5th Cir.1997).

Grove v. City of York, Pennsylvania, Civil No. 1:05-CV-02205, in F.Supp.2d, 2007 WL 465568 (M.D.Pa.)(not reported).

Guyer v. The School Board of Alachua County, Florida, 634 So.2d 806 (Fl.D.1st, 1994).

Holman v. Illinois, Not Reported in N.E.2d, 47 Ill.Ct.Cl. 372, 1995 WL 902088 (Ill.Ct.Cl.)

Hayward v. Carraway, 180 So.2d 758 (La.App., 1965).

116

Jordan v. Oakwood Homes, 167 N.C. App.371, 2004).

Kaplan v. Alpha Epsilon Phi, 42 N.W.2d 342, (Minn.,1950).

Mays v. Gretna, 668 So.2d 1207, 95-717 (La.App., 5th Cir.1996).

Nautilus v. Gardner (E.D.Pa. 2005) Not Reported in F.Supp.2d, 2005 WL 664358 (E.D.Pa.).

O'Bryan v. State, 591 S.W.2d 464 (Tex.Cr.App., 1979).

Policeman's Benefit Association v. Nautilus Insurance Company, No. M2001-00611-COA-R3-CV, 2002 WL 126311 (Tenn.Ct.App. Feb.1, 2002).

Powell v. Jacor Communications, 320 F.3d 599 (6th Cir.2003).

Purtell v. Mason, 527 F.3d 615 (7th Cir. 2008).

Salama v. Deaton, 10-CA-00310 (Fla. 13th Cir. Ct.), Amended Complaint (2010).

Seipp v. Wake County Board of Education, No. COA98-320, 1999 WL 20518 (N.C. Ct. App. Jan. 19, 1999).

Stambovsky v. Ackley, 169 A.D.2d 254 (NY App. Div. 1991).

State v. Erickson, 449 N.W.2d 707 (Minn.,1989).

Travis v. Robbins-Sykes Hardwood Flooring, 1993 Ark. App. LEXIS 617 (Nov. 17, 1993).

United States v. Modesto, 43 M.J. 315, 39 M.J. 1055(aff'd)(1995), Court of Appeals for the Armed Forces, No. 94–1213 (aff'd) (Sept 29, 1995).

Western World Ins. Co. v. Markel American Ins. Co. 677 F.3d 1266, C.A.10 (Okla. 2012).

Whimsicality, Inc. v. Rubie's Costume Co., 721 F. Supp. 1566, 1568 (E.D.N.Y. 1989) (Dearie, J.), affirmed in part vacated and remanded in part, 891 F.2d 452 (2d Cir. 1989), decision on remand, 1993 WL 460588 (E.D.N.Y. Nov. 4, 1993).

BIBLIOGRAPHY

Chapter 1 Introduction to Halloween Law
Ryan A. Malphurs, Ph.D.,"The Function of Laughter at the U.S. Supreme Court," 10 Communication L.R. 48-75 (2006).

Chapter 3 Halloween Property Law
Malla Pollack, "A Rose is a Rose is a Rose --- but is a Costume a Dress? An Alternative Solution in Whimsicality, Inc., v. Rubie's Costume Co., 41 J. Copyright Soc'y U.S.A. 1 (Fall, 1993).

Chapter 4 Halloween Contract Law
Daniel Moar, "Case Law from the Crypt," New York State Bar Association Journal 10-17 (Oct. 2011) at http://www.nysba.org/AM/Template.cfm?Section=Home &Template=/CM/ContentDisplay.cfm&ContentID=55814

Chapter 5 Halloween Criminal Law
Best, Joel and Gerald T. Horiuchi, "The Razor Blade in the Apple: The Social Construction of Urban Legends Source," 32 Social Problems 488-499 (Jun., 1985). http://www.jstor.org/stable/800777?origin=JSTOR-pdf

Eugene W. Fields, "New Halloween law bars sex offenders," The Orange County Register, Oct. 28, 2010 at http://www.ocregister.com/articles/law-273245-offenders-sex.html .

M. Benjamin Snodgrass, The Specter of Sex Offenders on Halloween: Unmasking Cultural, Constitutional and Criminological Concerns, 71 Ohio St. L.J. 417 (2010).

Katherine Ramsland, "The Fearful Vampire Killers," http://www.trutv.com/library/crime/serial_killers/weir d/vampires/1.html.

119

Chapter 7 Halloween Tort Law
Michele Angermiller, "Website helping Hamilton fire victim overcome injuries from Halloween costume fire," Trenton Times (Dec. 11, 2011).at http://www.nj.com/mercer/index.ssf/2011/12/website_helping_kitchen_hamilt.html

Nathan Duke, "Woman sues store over clown shoe fall," *New York Post* (Mar. 11, 2010). http://www.nypost.com/p/news/local/queens/woman_sues_store_over_clown_shoe_2i47M0tT8kcA03ltNKeViM#ixzz24j51DYvX

Johnathan Turley, "Res ipsa loquitur," blog, http://jonathanturley.org/2011/10/31/spooky-torts-the-2011-list-halloween-cases-and-controversies/ (Oct 31, 2011).

Chapter 8 Halloween Employment Law
Kim Bell, "Halloween haunted house worker found hanging from noose," St. Louis Post-Dispatch (Sat, 10/29/2011) at http://www.standard.net/stories/2011/10/29/halloween-haunted-house-worker-found-hanging-noose.

Chapter 9 Halloween Oil and Gas Law
Julie Carr Smyth with Thomas J. Sheeran, Associated Press, Cleveland, OH, "Gas under graveyards raises moral, money questions," June 30, 2012 at http://www.sfgate.com/news/article/Gas-under-graveyards-raises-moral-money-questions-3675826.php#page-2

Chapter 10 Halloween State and Local Government Law
Photo used with permission from Alan Pavilik, Hollywood, CA: http://www.smosh.com/smosh-pit/articles/6-insanely-ridiculous-halloween-laws

"6 Insanely Ridiculous Halloween Laws" at http://www.smosh.com/smosh-pit/articles/6-insanely-ridiculous-halloween-laws . Daniela Altimari, "State Lawmaker wants to tamper with tradition to ensure the holiday is always marked on a weekend," The Hartford Courant, Oct. 24, 2011 at http://articles.courant.com/2011-10-24/news/hc-a-state-lawmaker-wants-to-tamper-with-tradition-to-ensure-the-holiday-is-always-marked-on-a-weekend-20111024_1_halloween-larson-top-holidays

Rehoboth Beach, Delaware ordinance. http://www.idiotlaws.com/cant-trick-or-treat-after-8pm/

Chapter 11 Halloween Education Law
Associated Press quoted in Digital Journal, "Schools take traditional halloween customs out of the classroom," Oct 28, 2011, at http://www.digitaljournal.com/article/313471#ixzz24hJ8ORP7.

Debra Cassens Weiss, "Teens lawyer threatens litigation over a teachers bad Halloween prank," ABA Journal, Sept. 15, 2011, at http://www.abajournal.com/news/article/teens_lawyer_threatens_litigation_over_a_teachers_bad_halloween_prank/

Chapter 12. Halloween Legal Ethics
"Baum firm reaches settlement with Attorney General, The New York Law Journal, March 22, 2012 at http://www.newyorklawjournal.com/PubArticleNY.jsp?id=1202546538145&Baum_Firm_Reaches_Settlement_With_Attorney_General

National Halloween Injury Law Firm, "Halloween Trick or Treat Safety Tips for Children & Parents," Schmidt and

Clark law firm at
http://www.schmidtandclark.com/halloween-injury-lawyer-lawsuit

ACKNOWLEDGMENTS

I am grateful to my friends and family who shared their thoughts and comments with me about the book. I want to sincerely thank my colleagues, Richard E. Rosen, Chris Kulander, Jorge Ramirez and my research assistant, Jessica Haseltine for reading parts of this manuscript.

I also thank the American Association of Law Libraries for their interest in my publications.

Thanks to Summer Sutton for her tireless efforts to design the perfect cover for this book.

And thanks also to Dennis E. Hackin for inspiring me to go "outside the box" of traditional legal scholarship to express the ideas in this book.

INDEX

———

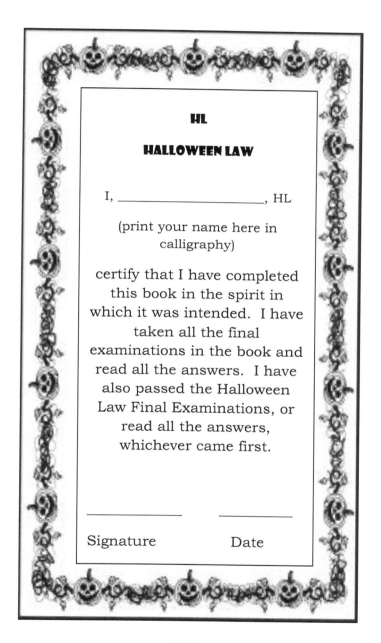

HL

HALLOWEEN LAW

I, _____, HL

(print your name here in
calligraphy)

certify that I have completed
this book in the spirit in
which it was intended. I have
taken all the final
examinations in the book and
read all the answers. I have
also passed the Halloween
Law Final Examinations, or
read all the answers,
whichever came first.

_____   _____

Signature   Date